Student's Federal Career Guide, 3rd Edition

Students, Recent Graduates, Veterans:
Learn how to write a competitive Federal Resume for a
Pathways Internship or USAJOBS Federal Career

By Kathryn Troutman and Paul Binkley
With contributions from Emily K. Troutman

The
Resume Place

Student's Federal Career Guide, 3rd Ed.

Printed in the United States of America
Copyright 2013 by Kathryn K. Troutman
ISBN 978-0-9846671-6-1
Library of Congress Control Number: 2012376245

Published by The Resume Place, Inc.
www.resume-place.com
Phone: (888) 480-8265 Fax: (410) 744 0119

We have been careful to provide accurate federal job search information in this book, but it is possible that errors or omissions may have been introduced as requirements change frequently.

Sample resumes are real but fictionalized. All federal applicants have given their permission for their resumes to be used as samples for the publication. Privacy policy is strictly enforced.

Book Credits

Publication Team

- → Cover Design: Brian Moore
- → Interior Page Design and Developmental Editing: Paulina Chen
- → Case Study Editors: Pamela Sikora, Amy Connelly, John Gagnon, and Ellen Lazarus
- → Contributor: John Gagnon
- → Student Internship Advisor: Emmanuel Waters
- → GI Bill Contributor: Mary Waring, George Washington University
- → Federal Human Resources Reviewer: Sandra Lee Keppley
- → Proofreaders: Pamela Sikora and Allison Goldstein
- → Co-Author for the First Edition and Contributor to the Second and Third Editions: Emily Troutman

TABLE OF CONTENTS

Sample Successful Resumes and Cover Letters

Student Veterans Resumes

TEN STEPS TO A FEDERAL JOB®
for Students and Recent Grads

Step 1: Research Federal Student Programs
What are Pathways programs? What other federal government opportunities are there for current students and recent graduates?

Step 2: Network
Don't think networking can help you? Think again!

Step 3: Find Your Agency, Job Title, and Grade
Get the tools you need to narrow down your job search.

Step 4: Search USAJOBS for Pathways Announcements
How to search 5,000 job postings for the perfect announcement for you.

Step 5: Analyze Vacancy Announcements
Learn how to interpret job announcements and successfully apply to federal positions appropriate for you.

Step 6: Write Your Federal Resume
The USAJOBS federal resume is longer than the traditional two-page private industry resume. Find out what you need to include in your resume.

Step 7: KSAs, Questionnaires, and Cover Letters
Give yourself all the credit you can in part 2 of your application.

Step 8: Submit Your Application
Avoid the most common mistakes when submitting your Pathways application in USAJOBS.

Step 9: Track and Follow Up
Don't just hit the send button and forget about your application. Following up can help you improve future submissions.

Step 10: Interview for a Federal Job
Get ready to tell your best stories about your accomplishments and leadership. Be personable, passionate about the job, and sharp. Get HIRED!

STEP 1: Research Federal Student Programs

Additional Student Veterans info on page 91

Pathways Internships for Students and Recent Grads

⇢ What are the best ways for students and recent graduates to enter the federal government?

⇢ What are the Pathways Programs? Which one is right for me?

⇢ How can I earn credit for my federal government experiences?

SAMPLE PATHWAYS ANNOUNCEMENT

Federal Student Programs

The following box shows the variety of programs you can consider.

> ⇢ The Pathways Programs
>   - Internship Program
>   - Recent Graduate Program
>   - Presidential Management Fellows Program
> ⇢ Student Volunteer Programs
> ⇢ Monetary Fellowships
> ⇢ Federal Work Study (FWS)
> ⇢ Summer Employment
> ⇢ Workforce Recruitment Program (WRP) for College Students with Disabilities
> ⇢ Professional and Technical Apprenticeships
> ⇢ Cooperatives (Co-ops)
> ⇢ Scholarships
> ⇢ Grants
> ⇢ Federal Service with Consulting Firms
> ⇢ Wounded Warrior Programs, Internships, and Apprenticeships (see page 96)

Start as early as possible. Finding and applying for federal job opportunities takes longer than you think.

Pathways Program Overview

The first step of any student or recent graduate's federal job search is to review what actual opportunities are available. You can search for Pathways internships easily on USAJOBS.gov.

Pathways Programs are available for students in high school through post-doctorate level.

The federal government recently implemented Pathways Programs, which are specifically targeted to current students and recent graduates. The Pathways framework is a group of two relatively new programs (the Internships and Recent Graduate Programs) and an update to a longstanding program (the Presidential Management Fellowship) aimed at recruiting students and recent graduates into federal service. The Pathways Programs are the new framework for students and recent graduates seeking federal jobs—to be successful in your search for a federal position, you absolutely must acquaint yourself with these programs.

At the very least, these programs offer you the chance to build a solid history of professional experience, "test drive" the federal government, build your federal network, and serve the public.

Key Points to Remember

1. **Know Your Interests:** Target agencies that interest you the most and network with people in those agencies.

2. **Proactively Search for Opportunities:** The most difficult part is simply finding these positions. Your first step should be to look on www.usajobs.gov; your second step to review agency websites; and your third step to review third party sites, such as that of Partnership for Public Service to see what offerings are available for students or recent graduates.

3. **It's Never Too Early to Start:** Federal hiring opportunities aimed at students often have application deadlines many months in advance of the start date. Some may require security clearances, which can take anywhere from four months to one year or more to perform. Others may have very short deadlines that pop up at inopportune times. You should start your research process early to allow time to find opportunities and to be prepared for those positions that suddenly appear.

What is Your Path?

The federal government recently revamped the way it recruits, hires, and trains students and recent graduates. In December 2010, President Obama signed Executive Order 13562 titled "Recruiting and Hiring Students and Recent Graduates."

The purpose of the Pathways Programs is to

> *...offer clear paths to Federal internships for students from high school through post-graduate school and to careers for recent graduates, and provide meaningful training and career development opportunities for individuals who are at the beginning of their Federal service.*

On July 10, 2012, a Final Rule implemented the regulations governing the Pathways Programs. For your research on these programs, take some time to review the information available at *www.opm.gov/HiringReform/Pathways*.

Under President Obama's leadership, the Federal Government has taken steps to help students and recent graduates join the Federal service. New opportunities will appear on USAJOBS as agencies post them. We encourage you to visit this site periodically, or set up a saved search.

Find Internships

Find Recent Graduate Jobs

www.usajobs.gov/StudentsandGrads

You can learn more about these programs at *www.usajobs.gov/StudentsandGrads* or by clicking "Students and Recent Graduates" under the USAJOBS Resource Center menu at *www.USAJOBS.gov*.

The Pathways Programs offer clear paths to Federal internships for students from high school through post-graduate school and to careers for recent graduates, and provide meaningful training and career development opportunities for individuals who are at the beginning of their Federal service. As a student or recent graduate, you can begin your career in the Federal government by choosing the path that best describes you and where you are in your academics:

⇢ **Internship Program:** This program is for current students enrolled in a wide variety of educational institutions from high school to graduate level, with paid opportunities to work in agencies and explore Federal careers while still in school. Additional information about the Internship Program can be found at *www.opm.gov/HiringReform/Pathways/program/interns/*.

⇢ **Recent Graduates Program:** This program is for individuals who have recently graduated from qualifying educational institutions or programs and seek a dynamic, career development program with training and mentorship. To be eligible, applicants must apply within two years of degree or certificate completion (except for veterans precluded from doing so due to their military service obligation, who will have up to six years to apply). Additional information about the Recent Graduates Program can be found at: *www.opm.gov/HiringReform/Pathways/program/graduates/*.

⇢ **Presidential Management Fellows Program:** For more than three decades, the PMF Program has been the Federal government's premier leadership development program for advanced degree candidates. This program is now for individuals who have received a qualifying advanced degree within the preceding two years. For complete program information visit: *www.pmf.gov*.

The federal government's new paradigm for current and recent students is designed to achieve a dual purpose: recruitment and development. With a wave of retirements across the federal government, as well as new technical issues involving national security concerns, the nation needs highly qualified, highly-skilled individuals to fill gaps and take on new roles. The Pathways Programs are designed to recruit young, talented people (like you!) and to develop them into the nation's next generation of world-class leaders and public servants.

A Few Words on Pathways, Excepted Service, and Conversion to Permanent Status

Before jumping into the details of the three prongs of the Pathways Programs, it is important to make a few general observations about how these programs are affected by different hiring authorities and government regulations. Most Pathways participants (including interns, recent graduates, and fellows) are considered "excepted service employees" which means that they 1) fall into a category of employees hired outside the competitive examination process and 2) are not considered permanent federal employees unless/until they are converted into the competitive service.

What does this mean for you? As a Pathways participant you may or may not be eligible for conversion to a permanent position in the competitive service. If this is important to you – and it should be – take great care to review the details of any Pathways announcement and to read the details of any Participant Agreement. This will help you know what to expect as you move forward with and complete your program. To learn more, spend some time perusing Office of Personnel's (OPM's) website, particularly the section on Hiring Authorities for Pathways participants.

In addition to the programs offered under the Pathways umbrella, some students may find opportunities in volunteer programs or temporary summer positions.

Internship Program

The Internship Program offers students from high school through college and graduate school opportunities to gain valuable federal experience while still in school. Prior to implementation of the Pathways Programs, many internships were posted disparately on a variety of job boards and federal agency websites. With the revamping of student hiring, now almost all internship opportunities can be found on www.usajobs.gov and on specific agency websites, which makes your search much easier.

The Office of Personnel Management outlines key aspects of the Internship Program, which you can view online (*www.opm.gov/policy-data-oversight/hiring-authorities/students-recent-graduates/#url=intern*). The major points are:

Eligibility

→ You must be a current student ("student" is an all-encompassing term that includes attendees of 4-year universities, community colleges, professional and vocational schools, graduate programs, and others). Be sure to review federal requirements for eligibility as a "current student," but if you are enrolled in an academic program leading to a degree or professional certification, it is likely that you qualify.

Internship Details

→ You can be hired temporarily for up to one year, or for an indefinite period pending completion of certain educational requirements.
→ You may be hired in either a full-time or part-time capacity.
→ You will sign a Participant Agreement with the agency detailing the expectations for the internship.
→ Your internship will be related to your career goals OR current field of study.

Completing the Internship

→ In some cases, you may be eligible for conversion into a permanent position straight from an internship! To be eligible for conversion, you have to meet certain specific requirements including: completing 640 hours of internship experience, completing your degree or certificate, and meeting other agency-mandated requirements. Agencies have wide latitude in exercising their discretionary authority in offering conversion opportunities to interns, so you'll need to review your specific agency's terms and the terms set forth in the Participant Agreement.

Recent Graduates Program

This program targets those who are about to graduate and those who recently graduated for developmental program positions in the federal government. These are full-time employment positions after graduation designed to help agencies recruit, train, and retain highly qualified individuals who may not have enough experience to be successful in the competitive hiring process. Here are the main points of the Recent Graduates program:

Eligibility

⇢ You must apply within two years of completing a degree or certificate. NOTE: if you are a veteran, in certain circumstances you can apply within six years of completing your studies.

Program Details

⇢ The program is designed to be dynamic and developmental in its focus, with a specific goal of preparing you for a federal career. The program lasts for one year (unless the training requirements of the position warrant a lengthier training period).

⇢ As part of the developmental focus of this program you will receive mentorship, an individual development plan, 40-hours of formal training, and career advancement opportunities.

⇢ You will sign a Participant Agreement with the agency.

Completing the Program

⇢ You may be converted to a permanent position if you successfully complete the requirements of the program, perform satisfactorily, and meet certain qualifications for the position.

You may be eligible to convert to a permanent position after completing your program!

Presidential Management Fellows (PMF) Program

The Presidential Management Fellows (PMF) program is the premiere federal recruiting program. Its purpose is to "attract to the federal service outstanding men and women from a variety of academic disciplines and career paths who have a clear interest in, and commitment to, excellence in the leadership and management of public policies and programs."

The PMF is designed to recruit and place highly-qualified advanced-degree holders into developmental opportunities for potential permanent conversion. Successful completion of the PMF is often a fast track to the upper levels of government, including the Senior Executive Service. During their two-year fellowship, PMFs receive rotational assignments and training opportunities intended to broaden their public leadership and management abilities.

Eligibility

→ You must have completed an advanced degree within the past two years (masters, professional degree, or higher).

Program Details

→ The PMF Program includes two years of developmental training and performance experience in the federal government.
→ You will receive a personal mentor, be placed in occupational and functional positions, and be offered 80+ hours of annual formal training.
→ You will be placed on a performance plan during your fellowship and must be rated as "successful" for each rating period to be able to continue in the program.

Completing the PMF

→ Once you complete your two years in the fellowship, you may be eligible for appointment into the competitive service. This is not guaranteed, but the program's goal is to develop future federal leaders. So, if you pay attention, do good work, take advantage of what the opportunity offers, network, and complete your trainings, you will probably be in good shape at the end of your fellowship. As always, make sure you read all your agreements and know the agency's specific terms of any of its offers for you.

For more details about the PMF Program, visit *www.pmf.gov*, which is the government's one-stop-shop for resources for current and potential Presidential Management Fellows.

Other Federal Student Opportunities

Student Volunteer Programs

OK, you're right—"volunteer" means without pay. Maybe that isn't for you. But if you've ever wanted to gain experience in a particular career field, or have been curious about what it's like to work for a particular federal agency, this is an opportunity for you to consider. If nothing else, it will give you the chance to have something to put in that "Professional Experience" block of your resume when you go after paying jobs. And don't forget, it is also a great opportunity to network and build professional relationships that can help you out later in your job search.

In general, federal agencies are not allowed to accept volunteer work, but there are exceptions to that legal prohibition. One of the exceptions is "employment of students to further their educational goals." Many federal agencies offer volunteer work to high school and college students. If you are curious about a particular agency or career field, or just want to get a feel for working for a federal agency, contact the agency or agencies that interest you.

> An unpaid volunteer position can give you the professional experience you need to land a paid position in the future.

The range of volunteer possibilities is astounding. You could be involved in professional projects or other work activities related to what you are studying. Considering how diverse the federal government is, it isn't too hard to realize you could work on anything from new administrative procedures to congressional relations to issues dealing with the environment or wildlife management. The actual work assignments performed by student volunteers are determined by the host agency.

You are eligible for student volunteer work if you are enrolled at least half-time in:
- an accredited high school or trade school
- a technical or vocational school
- a junior or community college
- a four-year college or university
- any other accredited educational institution

Monetary Fellowships

Monetary fellowships are usually federally-funded research or study opportunities. They vary widely. Some fellowships operate like scholarship funds (or grants) with academic requirements but no actual job in government. Many of these fellowships focus on students interested in specific areas of study such as the American Chemical Society Congressional Fellowship Program, the Charles B. Rangel International Affairs Fellowship, or the U.S. Department of Education Jacob K. Javits Fellowship Program.

There may be many more of these fellowships throughout the federal government. To find out more, search agency websites and talk with your institution's Financial Aid office.

Federal Work Study (FWS)

Not many agencies would pass up the opportunity to hire great student workers at only 25% of their hourly rate. And very few college students would pass up the opportunity to gain valuable federal experience and get paid a decent wage.

Federal Work Study (FWS) offers these and other advantages to both federal agencies and students. Sadly, much of the FWS funds are not used by students because they do not know what it could mean for their professional development.

The original purpose of the FWS program was to get students working in the communities around their colleges and universities. Today, many students, undergraduate and graduate, are eligible for FWS if they receive federal financial support for their education.

FWS jobs may be on or off campus. Off-campus FWS positions can be with federal, state, or local public agencies, or nonprofit organizations, and they must be positions that serve the public interest.

Characteristics of FWS:
- Eligibility determined by the amount of student need
- Undergraduate and graduate students attending Title IV funding eligible institutions of higher education are eligible (includes community colleges, vocational colleges, professional schools, etc.)
- Students must be paid an hourly wage that is at least equal to the federal minimum wage
- Students receive a bi-weekly check from their school which means, in most cases, the hiring agency does not technically hire the student
- The hiring agency pays only a portion of the wage, usually around 25-30%, and the remainder comes from federal funds allocated to the institution
- Students may also earn academic credit for their FWS position
- Depending on their school's rules, FWS students can work at any time during the calendar year, and they can work anywhere in the United States, and sometimes abroad

FWS is administered differently by every school and, therefore, you must check with your career center and financial aid office for more information. You can also learn more about FWS by visiting the U.S. Department of Education's website at *www.ifap.ed.gov/ifap/*, the Campus Compact website (*www.compact.org*), or by searching for "FWS."

Many agencies may not know about FWS, which can be a positive and a negative for students. Introducing an agency to FWS would show great foresight, help you make contacts at that agency, and possibly lead to a FWS position for you. The negative, however, is that implementing a new program like this in the federal government often takes more time than you may have.

Being proactive is one of the best ways to build a strong professional network and to create future opportunities for yourself. Therefore, have the appropriate information on FWS ready to present to agency hiring managers.

Workforce Recruitment Program (WRP)

The Workforce Recruitment Program for College Students with Disabilities (WRP) is a recruitment and referral program that connects federal and private sector employers nationwide with highly motivated college students and recent graduates with disabilities who are eager to prove their abilities in the workplace through summer or permanent jobs.

What Does the WRP Offer to Eligible Students and Recent Graduates?
The WRP is an excellent way for students and recent graduates with disabilities to:
⇢ Market their abilities to a wide variety of potential employers across the United States
⇢ Sharpen their interviewing skills during a required phone interview with a WRP recruiter
⇢ Gain valuable skills, experience, and contacts on the job
⇢ Prove that people with disabilities can be excellent employees

Welcome to the 2011 Workforce Recruitment Program for College Students with Disabilities (WRP)

If you are an Employer in the federal government and wish to take advantage of WRP,
Register Now!
If you are a private sector employer and wish to take advantage of WRP, go to www.askEARN.org.
If you're a school or student interested in WRP and wish to learn more, read our About Us section for more details.

Do you need highly qualified candidates for jobs at your office? The Workforce Recruitment Program can help! The WRP is a recruitment and referral program that connects federal and private sector employers nationwide with highly motivated postsecondary students and recent graduates with disabilities who are eager to prove their abilities in the workplace through summer or permanent jobs. Co-sponsored by the U.S. Department of Labor's Office of Disability Employment Policy (ODEP) and the U.S. Department of Defense with the participation of many other federal agencies and sub-agencies, the WRP has provided employment opportunities for over 5,500 students since 1995.

Annually, trained WRP recruiters from federal agencies conduct personal interviews with interested students on college and university campuses across the country. Students represent all majors, and range from college freshmen to graduate students and law students. Information from these student interviews is compiled in a searchable database that is available through this website to federal Human Resources Specialists, Equal Employment Opportunity Specialists, and other hiring officials in federal agencies. You can request a password here. If you are an employer in the private sector, or a student interested in private sector employment, you can take advantage of the WRP program through the National Employer Technical Assistance Center at www.askEARN.org. or call toll-free 1-855-275-3276.

sign in
email
password
Sign In
Forgot your password?

Disclaimer: This is a U.S. Government computer system. U.S. Government computer systems are provided for the processing of Official U.S. Government information only. All information contained on this system is owned by the Department of Labor and the Department of Defense and may be monitored, intercepted, recorded, read, copied, or captured in any manner and disclosed in any manner, by authorized personnel.

www.wrp.gov

How Does a Student Become an "Eligible Student" for the WRP Database?

To register, you must go through your university or college Student Disability Services Office. Your university or college must be a member of the WRP in order to you to list your resume in the WRP database. If your university or college is not a member of the WRP, you can join through a different university that is a member of WRP. There are currently only 300 university members of the WRP. You can encourage your career center to become a member of WRP.

⋯→ Deadlines for registration: Eligible candidates must contact your Student Disability Services Office early in the Spring semester to be considered for inclusion into the WRP.

⋯→ Candidates must follow through with the campus coordinators to ensure successful completion of the online application process and any additional requirements that the campus coordinator has put in place.

⋯→ Follow the resume formats in this book for submission of your resume to the WRP database. Follow the instructions for your Schedule A letter from the Check Sheet on this webpage: http://www.dol.gov/odep/wrp/Students.htm

⋯→ Phone Interviews are conducted in October and early November.

For more information on the WRP, visit *www.wrp.gov*, or contact your school's Disabilities Support Services or Career Services Center.

Top 10 Occupations for Fiscal Year 2012

Registered Apprenticeship has over 1,000 apprenticeable occupation traditionally strong showing in the construction industry. Here are ou which are available in both Green industries and growing industries.

Top 10 Occupations for Fiscal Year 2012	
Occupation Title	Active Apprentices
Electrician	36,742
Carpenter	15,479
Plumber	13,201
Pipe Fitter	8,586
Contruction Craft Laborer	7,947
Sheet Metal Worker	7,714
Roofer	5,479
Structural Steel/Ironworker	5,041
Painter	3,560
Pipe Fitter (Sprinkler Fitter)	3,266

DATA NOTE: The data in this table is from the Registered Apprentice The system includes data for the 25 Office of Apprenticeship (OA) st

Professional and Technical Apprenticeships

The government does have an apprentice program for skilled crafts and trades occupations, generally referred to as trades or blue-collar jobs. Some of these programs are very limited in their geographic or organizational reach. They cover both high school and college students. Information about these programs is available at the website for the Department of Labor's Employment and Training Administration (*www.doleta.gov/OA/*).

Federal apprenticeships operate as formal programs, combining theory and practice in the work performed. Completion of the program qualifies the individual as a journeyman in the field of the apprenticeship, such as an electrician or carpenter.

While the number of these federal trades jobs is shrinking, replacements are still needed. Applicants for these federal apprenticeships follow normal competitive employment processes, including taking a test.

www.doleta.gov/OA/

Successful completion of an apprenticeship is often equivalent to a two-year degree, and qualifies the individual for the career field without further education.

Federal trades employees are paid at least as much as, and often more than, their privately employed, unionized counterparts, and usually have better benefits packages. Fully competent federal trades employees have salary growth as journeymen and potential to be promoted into work leader and supervisor jobs, including foreman positions.

Apprentice programs vary by agency and location. You can search for federal trade apprenticeship opportunities on the USAJOBS website or on agency websites (look particularly at the armed forces departments, especially Navy, and the departments of Agriculture, the Interior, Veterans Affairs, and the General Services Administration).

Scholarships

An amazing number of federal organizations offer scholarships. Some focus on minority or disadvantaged students, some are for graduate or postgraduate work, and some require entering the armed forces. Often the purpose of these programs is to help students pay for the education and build their experience level by agreeing to work at that agency after they graduate. To find more information on scholarships, visit agency websites and search for "scholarships."

Cooperatives (Co-ops)

Cooperative Education (aka Co-ops) programs are similar to apprenticeships in that the purpose of these experiences is to give students the opportunity to apply the theory they learn in the classroom to real-world settings. As with apprenticeships, companies partner with schools in Co-op programs intending to hire students after they finish their academic requirements. The federal government enters into these arrangements with colleges and universities to give students a chance to combine their classroom studies with on-the-job training.

The main difference between these two programs is that Co-op students attend class while they work; apprenticeships usually do not include a classroom component. Students earn academic credit toward their degrees for their Co-op experiences, and they appear on students' official transcripts.

The balance between classroom and work in cooperative education varies by the school. Sometimes Co-op students work three days a week and attend classes two days a week. Other institutions prefer that Co-op students alternate working full-time an entire term with attending classes full-time the other term.

For more information about cooperative education, contact your Career Center.

Grants

The *www.usajobs.gov/StudentsandGrads* website also has a link for grants. Grants are an especially important opportunity for students conducting specialized research, which often means students pursuing advanced degrees.

Federal Service with Consulting Firms

Another entry point for students into federal service is to intern or work with for-profit (and a few not-for-profit) consulting firms. There are a huge number of contractors working for the federal government. Management consulting companies are a subset of this group that work with federal agencies to strategize, plan, implement, staff, and evaluate the programs and projects needed to serve the public. Many of these organizations, large and small, offer internship opportunities for undergraduate and graduate students. The main purpose of these programs is for both the company and the student to "test drive" each other. These internships are very competitive and often lead to full-time employment after graduation.

Companies that may offer these types of internships include Booz Allen Hamilton, Deloitte Consulting, IBM Consulting, LMI Government Consulting, KPMG, Accenture, and Ernst & Young. Contact your Career Center for more information or contact the consulting company directly. Networking with alumni of your school is an excellent way to learn more about these internship programs and to find employment.

STEP 2: Network

*Additional Student Veterans
info on page 91*

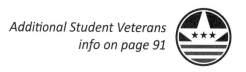

Top Questions to Ask in an Informational Interview with a Federal Employee or Manager

→ How did you find your position?
→ What education or experience is necessary for a job like yours?
→ What kind of a job would people in your position look for next?
→ How do you spend an average day at work?
→ What skills or attributes do you consider crucial to your job?
→ What aspects of your job do you love/dislike?
→ What other agencies do you work with?
→ To which professional associations would someone in your field belong?
→ Can you recommend someone else whom I might interview?

SAMPLE PATHWAYS ANNOUNCEMENT

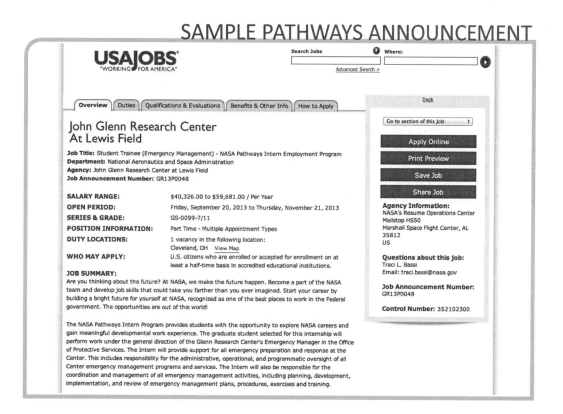

NETWORKING BASICS

Why Network?

For many students, finding a summer job or internship means canvassing internet job boards or contacting many managers of businesses or organizations to gain information. Networking is just a sophisticated, efficient form of these searches.

This step is more important than you may realize. The federal government is huge, and the hiring process is both complex and decentralized. Visualize the federal government as an iceberg (generally huge and imposing!), which you can see only a small part of at one time.

Networking will help in several ways as you navigate federal hiring. You will 1) become familiar with the hiring process; 2) learn of unposted and upcoming jobs; and 3) find the best matches for your interests.

Your networking contacts may work with a little-known agency that would be perfect for you. For instance, have you ever heard of the National Geospatial Intelligence Agency or the Southern European Task Force? Agency names also change, and the hiring processes of new federal entities, like the Consumer Financial Protection Bureau, can be especially challenging to navigate.

How to Network

The most visible federal government employees are often the least accessible, such as those featured on television. The people in such jobs are also politically appointed, not hired. Political appointees make up only about 0.001% of all federal jobs! As a student or recent graduate, you probably want to set your sights on more behind-the-scenes positions. Here are some basic strategies to make the task less daunting:

- ⤑ Start with people you know
- ⤑ Don't be embarrassed to ask your friends and family for assistance
- ⤑ Now is the time to call up your long lost Uncle Fritz and let him know you are in the market for a federal job. He may not work in the federal government, but he likely can point you in the direction of someone who does
- ⤑ Tap into your alumni network to find current federal employees who share a connection with your school

WHERE TO NETWORK

Your Career Services Office

The career services office of your school can provide you with many different services as a student or alum. Many career services offices now manage comprehensive career management websites – a good place to start when looking for a job opportunity. Additionally, they typically offer the following services to assist you:

- Resume development/feedback
- Career workshops
- Interview coaching (Informational, Behavioral, Case, etc.)
- Job search tools/strategies
- Dress-for-success tips
- Alumni and other connections
- One-on-one career counseling
- Employer information
- Self-assessment tools
- Career days/fairs
- Mentoring
- Co-ops/Apprenticeships

Professional Associations

There are hundreds of professional associations and groups in the United States, representing every single occupation and particular facets of an occupation. Internet searches are a good way to start, but for a comprehensive list of associations in your field, you should consult your career services office or local reference librarian. Libraries usually own one or more directories of professional associations, which list every possible group and give information about how to join.

Most associations offer low-cost student memberships with great benefits like workshops, newsletters, job bulletin boards, and member lists. Member phone and e-mail lists can be a great way to contact people and conduct informational interviews. Two places to find information on associations around the world are Weddles (*www.weddles.com/associations*), and ASAE—The Center for Association Leadership (*www.careerhq.org*).

Your Academic Program

Federal employers often develop relationships directly with college professors or departments (School of Business, Engineering, etc.). These relationships are encouraged by the college or university and offer opportunities to enhance placement for the best and the brightest—because the candidates are clearly visible to professors and instructors. Many employers will work with the individual college to provide career information, student briefings, and coaches and mentors.

Alumni and Alumni Associations

Every college or university has an alumni association. Most colleges rely heavily on alumni groups to act as coaches and mentors, provide fund raising for scholarships, and offer job opportunities to current students. College alumni may have a better understanding of your curriculum and can give you insightful, directed career advice. The easiest way to find alumni groups is through the career services office or your college or university's website.

Online Networking

LinkedIn is an ideal social medium, not only for networking, but also for learning about organizations, initiating professional discussions, gaining answers to your professional questions, and building your brand. One of the best features on LinkedIn is Groups. Many professional and alumni associations have created groups on LinkedIn. If you are a member of a group with someone, you can directly connect with other group members without an introduction from one of your contacts. Groups are also a fantastic way to get connected to those professional associations that interest you the most. Odds are that your school has an alumni association group on LinkedIn. Take advantage of the fact that alumni want to help current students and other alumni. And when it's time, you can help others, too.

You can also follow federal agencies on LinkedIn. That means when any of your connections change positions in the federal government or new contacts are announced, you will know about them as they are posted to LinkedIn.

GovLoop is another important site for those working in the government and those hoping to get a federal position. GovLoop is almost the LinkedIn for the federal government sector. Check it out at *www.govloop.com*.

Surveys of private industry hiring professionals show that as many as 90% use social media in screening prospective employees.

Sample LinkedIn Profile

Our sample LinkedIn profile goes with the real resume sample for Emmanuel Willis found on page 119. See the entire LinkedIn sample at http://www.linkedin.com/pub/emmanuel-willis/88/327/458.

Linked in ®

Emmanuel Willis

MBA Recent Graduate at Texas A&M University

Tulsa, Oklahoma (Tulsa, Oklahoma Area) | Government Administration

Join LinkedIn and access Emmanuel Willis's full profile. It's free!

As a LinkedIn member, you'll join 250 million other professionals who are sharing connections, ideas, and opportunities.

- See who you and **Emmanuel Willis** know in common
- Get introduced to **Emmanuel Willis**
- Contact **Emmanuel Willis** directly

View Emmanuel's full profile

Emmanuel Willis's Overview

Past	MBA Recent Graduate at Texas A&M University
	Technician/Customer Service Specialist at ACER Networking America
	Educational Program Technician at Child Development Center
	see all ▾
Education	Texas A&M University
	Oral Roberts University
Connections	**0 connections**

Emmanuel Willis' Summary

Seeking an international public service opportunity with specializations in business, contracts, technology and international communications.

Proficient in Microsoft Word, Excel, Java, C++, Cisco, Networking 1, and PowerPoint. Demonstrated website development and management experience.

Emmanuel Willis' Experience

MBA Recent Graduate

Texas A&M University

Educational Institution; 10,001+ employees; Higher Education industry

September 2009 – May 2012 (2 years 9 months) | Commerce, Texas

SENIOR PAPER TEAM PROJECT: Consisted of three team members taking a local owned business and preparing a 75-page research paper. Each member of the team took a section of the project which consisted of 25 pages of research, i.e., surveys, Strength, Weakness, Opportunities, and Threat analysis (SWOT), confidential company financials, financial ratios, new proposed marketing plan, and supply chain analysis. Resulted in implementation of 82% of the findings. Reduced debt ratio for the business by ten percent.

STRATEGIC MANAGEMENT TEAM PROJECT: Researched major Fortune 500 national grocery chain and prepared a 130-page analysis of the overall status of the company. Analyzed complex industry to determine where company could become more effective and profitable. Researched key information such as general economic conditions, top competitors, supply chain, value chain analysis, competitive strength assessments, and internal analysis. Submitted new business ideas, strategies, and proposed business plan to the grocery chain for acquisition, negotiation of contracts for property rentals, and expansion mergers locally and nationally.

INTERNATIONAL BUSINESS PROJECT: Compared economies in emerging markets of Brazil, Russia, India, and China. Researched similarities and differences such as Gross Domestic Product, purchasing power parity, exchange rates, real growth rate and local trading agreements or organizations, and contract negotiations among the four. Organized, planned and presented 75-minute presentation with question and answer period to peers and raters. A current UN delegate to Afghanistan was present and attempted to recruit for employment opportunities after presentation.

FINANCIAL MANAGEMENT PROJECT: Independent project which was required to be completed under strict time constraints. Compared the overall financial status of Dell and Apple. Analyzed profit margin, debt ratios, stocks, bonds, annuities, inventory ratio and net income, and net loss.

Technician/Customer Service Specialist

ACER Networking America

September 2007 – September 2008 (1 year 1 month) | Tulsa, Oklahoma

Helped network and troubleshoot all Acer desktops and laptops. Provided great customer care and service for Acer customers. Upheld all company regulations and Code of Business Conduct by enforcing loss prevention policies and communicating violations to the supervisory team. Assisted management team in establishing goals and priorities of staff.

Reported customer feedback and provided input in direct services to maximize productivity standards to upper management. Individualized marketing and sales strategy resulting in record local net profit. A strong participant in team selling. Handled competitive situation with competence and tact. Skilled in refusing customer requests while presenting alternative solutions. Modeled and encouraged a healthy work environment amongst staff brand associates, achieving first rate team dynamics.

STEP 3: Find Your Agency, Job Title, and Grade

Additional Student Veterans info on page 91

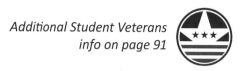

Follow Your Personal Mission Statement

⇢ What agencies do the things that interest me?

⇢ Which job titles are right for me?

⇢ How do I figure out which grades I can qualify for in the federal government?

SAMPLE PATHWAYS ANNOUNCEMENT

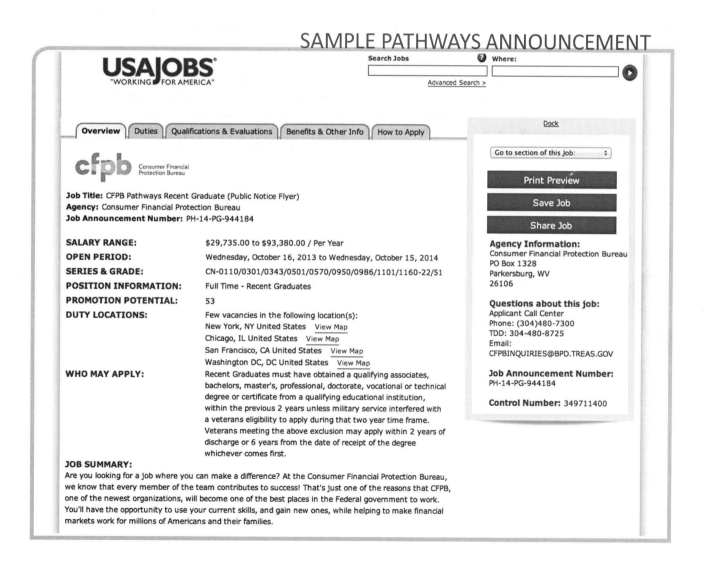

USAJOBS "WORKING FOR AMERICA"

Search Jobs   Where: Advanced Search >

Overview | Duties | Qualifications & Evaluations | Benefits & Other Info | How to Apply

cfpb Consumer Financial Protection Bureau

Job Title: CFPB Pathways Recent Graduate (Public Notice Flyer)
Agency: Consumer Financial Protection Bureau
Job Announcement Number: PH-14-PG-944184

SALARY RANGE: $29,735.00 to $93,380.00 / Per Year
OPEN PERIOD: Wednesday, October 16, 2013 to Wednesday, October 15, 2014
SERIES & GRADE: CN-0110/0301/0343/0501/0570/0950/0986/1101/1160-22/51
POSITION INFORMATION: Full Time - Recent Graduates
PROMOTION POTENTIAL: 53
DUTY LOCATIONS: Few vacancies in the following location(s):
New York, NY United States   View Map
Chicago, IL United States   View Map
San Francisco, CA United States   View Map
Washington DC, DC United States   View Map
WHO MAY APPLY: Recent Graduates must have obtained a qualifying associates, bachelors, master's, professional, doctorate, vocational or technical degree or certificate from a qualifying educational institution, within the previous 2 years unless military service interfered with a veterans eligibility to apply during that two year time frame. Veterans meeting the above exclusion may apply within 2 years of discharge or 6 years from the date of receipt of the degree whichever comes first.

JOB SUMMARY:
Are you looking for a job where you can make a difference? At the Consumer Financial Protection Bureau, we know that every member of the team contributes to success! That's just one of the reasons that CFPB, one of the newest organizations, will become one of the best places in the Federal government to work. You'll have the opportunity to use your current skills, and gain new ones, while helping to make financial markets work for millions of Americans and their families.

Dock

Go to section of this Job:

Print Preview

Save Job

Share Job

Agency Information:
Consumer Financial Protection Bureau
PO Box 1328
Parkersburg, WV
26106

Questions about this job:
Applicant Call Center
Phone: (304)480-7300
TDD: 304-480-8725
Email:
CFPBINQUIRIES@BPD.TREAS.GOV

Job Announcement Number:
PH-14-PG-944184

Control Number: 349711400

What Agency Will Be Right for You?

To select an agency of interest to you, follow these three steps:
1. Create a "mission statement match"
2. Consider location preferences
3. Know what's hot

Mission Statement Match

Pursuing a career in federal public service gives you the opportunity to choose an agency with a mission that matches yours. This is a great privilege and one of the many underrated and unrecognized benefits of working for the federal government.

A mission statement is an organization's vision of its purpose and work philosophy. Mission statements are often a practical guide and contain valuable information about each agency's goals, structure, and culture. Craft a professional mission statement for yourself and use that as a benchmark for evaluating federal employment opportunities. What are your goals, interests, and skills? What do you want to accomplish for your nation?

You can use your network to better understand agency missions, services, and customers. To find mission statements, visit the homepage of any federal agency. Review missions statements from a range of agencies to find your "best fit" for federal employment. Ask yourself how you can help achieve mission success and – even more importantly – whether you'd be happy working in an agency's articulated environment. Compare your professional mission statement with that of the agency's – how close is the match?

 Contrary to popular belief, most federal jobs are NOT located in Washington, D.C. As you begin your search, find out which agencies are based in your city.

11 Hottest College Majors

U.S. News and World Report's Cathie Gandel writes about 11 Hot College Majors (September 10, 2013). These hot majors are translated into real government job titles, occupational series, and typical agencies that may recruit and hire for related internships or positions.

1. Biomedical Engineering
→ Government Positions: 1. Clinical Engineer (Biomedical),
   2. Interdisciplinary Engineer General/Electronics/Biomedical,
   3. Electrician Engineer (Biomedical)
→ Series: GS-0855, GS-0856, and GS-0858
→ Departments: Army, Health and Human Services, and Veterans Affairs

2. Biometrics
→ Government Positions: 1. Operations Research Analyst, 2. Physical Security Specialist,
   3. Special Agent, 4. Management and Program Analyst
→ Series: GS-1515, GS-0080, GS-1800, GS-0343
→ Departments: Homeland Security, Defense, Federal Bureau of Investigation

3. Forensic Science
→ Government Positions: 1. Law Enforcement Specialist, 2. Chemist 3. Medical Officer 4. Medical Technician
→ Series: GS-1801, GS-1320, GS-0602, GS-0645
→ Departments: Homeland Security, Defense, Veterans Affairs, Federal Bureau of Investigation

4. Computer Game Design
→ Government Positions: 1. Computer Scientist, 2. Computer Engineer, 3. Electronics Engineer
→ Series: DP-1550-02, GS-0854
→ Departments: Navy, Naval Air Systems Command: Air Force

5. Cybersecurity
→ Government Positions: 1. Intelligence Operations Specialist, 2. Chief Assurance information Officer, 3. Intelligence Officer
→ Series: GS-0132, SL-2210
→ Departments: National Security Agency, Treasury, Defense Intelligence Agency

6. Data Science
- Government Positions: 1. Data Analyst, 2. Data Validator, 3. IT Specialist, 4. Program Analyst
- Series: NF-0343, GS-0675, GS-2210, GS-0343
- Departments: Commerce, Environment Protection Agency, Consumer Financial Protection Bureau

7. Business Analytics
- Government Positions: 1. Business Opportunity Specialist, 2. Business Applications Manager, 3. Administrative Specialist
- Series: GS-1101, ES-0340, GS-1801
- Departments: Small Business Administration, Health and Human Services, General Services Administration

8. Petroleum Engineering
- Government Positions: 1. Petroleum Engineer, 2. Engineering Technician, 3. Geologist/ Geophysicist
- Series: GS-0881, GS-0802, GS-1313
- Departments: Department of the Interior, Bureau of Indian Affairs, Department of Defense

9. Public Health
- Government Positions: 1. Public Health Advisor, 2. Health System Specialist
- Series: GS-0671, GS-0685
- Departments: Army, Health and Human Services

10. Robotics
- Government Positions: 1. Computer Engineer, 2. Research Materials Engineer
- Series: GS-0854, GS-0806
- Departments: Defense, National Aeronautics and Space Administration

11. Sustainability
- Government Positions: 1. Industrial Engineer, 2. Soil Scientist, 3. Ecological Specialist
- Series: GS-0896, GS-0454, GS-0408
- Departments: Veterans Affairs, Agriculture, Environmental Protection Agency

---

Report from:
www.usnews.com/education/best-colleges/articles/2013/09/10/discover-11-hot-college-majors-that-lead-to-jobs

Find Your Federal Job Chart

MAJOR	FEDERAL JOB TITLES
Accounting	Accounting Specialist, Budget Analyst, Contract Specialist, Auditor, Cost Accountant, Financial Analyst
Aerospace Engineering	Aerospace Engineering, Safety Engineer, Materials Engineer
Agricultural Engineering	Agricultural Engineer, Range Technician, Safeguarding, Intervention, Trade Compliance Officer
American Studies	Researcher, Writer-Editor, Policy Analyst, Program & Mgt. Analyst
Ancient and Medieval Art and Archaeology	Cryptanalyst, Intelligence Analyst, Clandestine Service
Ancient Near Eastern Studies	Cryptanalyst, Intelligence Analyst, Special Agent, Clandestine Service
Animal Sciences	Wildlife Biologist, Animal Scientist
Arabic	Foreign Languages, Cryptanalyst, Intelligence Analyst, Special Agent, Toponymist
Art History	Cryptanalyst, Special Agent, Intelligence Analyst, Archives Specialist
Asian Languages and Literatures	Foreign Language Studies, Cryptanalyst, Special Agent, Passport Officer
Biology	Biological Science Group, Forensic Chemist, Imagery Intelligence Analyst, Fishery Biologist
Biomedical Engineering	Biomedical Engineer, Research Ecologist Rhizosphere
Botany Biosystems and Agricultural Engineering	Safeguarding, Intervention & Trade Compliance Officer, Plant Protection and Quarantine Officer, Assistant Manager, Plant Materials Center (NRCS)
Business Administration	Contract Specialist, Acquisitions, Business & Industry Series, Supply Analyst, Grants and Agreements Speciaist (Forest Service), Realty Specialist, Restructuring Analyst, Inventory Management Specialist, Industrial Security Specialist
Cell and Development Biology	National Institutes of Health (NIH) Researcher
Chemical Engineering and Materials Science	Chemical Engineering and Materials Science
Chemistry	Chemist, Physical Scientist, Forensic Chemist, Imagery Intelligence Analyst
Civil Engineering	Civil Engineer, Construction Representative
Classical and Near Eastern Studies	Cryptanalyst, Special Agent, Intelligence Analyst, Clandestine Service
Clinical Laboratory Science	NIH Clinical Research Positions
Communication Studies	Writer-Editor, Public Affairs Specialist, Program & Management Analyst
Computer Engineering	Info Tech Specialist, Project Manager, Program Manager, Computer Scientist, Telecom Specialist
Computer Science & Information Sciences	Quality Assurance Specialist, Patent Examiner (Electrical & Computer Engineering, Computer Science)
Conservation Biology	Biologist, Ecologist, Wildlife Refuge Manager, Environmental Protection Specialist
Construction Management	Facilities Management Specialist, Realty Specialist

Find Your Federal Job Chart

MAJOR	FEDERAL JOB TITLES
Creative Writing	Writer-Editor, Public Affairs Specialist, Program & Management Analyst, Speechwriter
Criminal Justice	Physical Security Specialist, Intelligence Operations Specialist, Security Specialist, Investigator
Crop, Soil, and Pest Management	Agronomist, Agriculture Extension, Entomologist, Soil Conservation, Soil Scientist
Cultural Studies	Cryptanalyst, Special Agent, Intelligence Analyst, Clandestine Service, Foreign Service Officer
East Asian Studies	Cryptanalyst, Special Agent, Intelligence Analyst, Clandestine Service
Ecology	Ecologist, Biologist, Fisheries Biologist, Wildlife Biologist, Physical Scientist
Economics	Economist, Statistician, Mathemetician, Imagery Intelligence Analyst, Economic Research Analyst
Education	Teacher, Training Specialist, Geospatial Intelligence Instructor, Education Specialist, Transformation Facilitator
Educational Policy and Administration	Policy Analyst, Program and Management Analyst, Legislative Analyst
Emergency Health Services	Emergency Preparedness, Emergency Services Dispatcher, Paramedic
Emergency Medical Technician	Firefighter, Emergency Medical Technician, Law Enforcement Communications Assistant, Disaster Recovery & Operations Specialist, Range Technician (Initial Attack Fire/Aviation Dispatcher), Occupational Safety & Health
English	Writer-Editor, Public Affairs Specialist, Program & Management Analyst, Legislative Analyst
English as a Second Language	ESOL Teacher, International Relations, Education Specialist
Environmental Science	Biologist, Ecologist, Wildlife Refuge Manager, Environmental Prot. Spec., Program Manager
Epidemiology	Epidemiologist
Finance	Financial Analyst, Financial Management Specialist, Auditor, Financial & Program Analyst
Fisheries and Wildlife	Fisheries Biologist, Wildlife Biologist, Biologist, Ecologist
Food Science	Researcher, Research Food Technologist/Chemist/Physical Scientist, Dietitian (Lipid/Cardiovascular Disease Specialist), Public Health Nutritionist, Consumer Safety Officer, Agricultural Program Specialist, Public Health Nutritionist-Dietitian
Forestry	Forester, Forestry Technician, Wildland Fire Program Manager
Geographic Information Science	GIS specialist - linked with scientific field (Biology. Geology), Regional ISMS/ GeoBOB Data Steward (interdisciplinary)

MAJOR	FEDERAL JOB TITLES
Global Studies	Environmental Protection Specialist, International Relations Specialist, Import Policy Analyst, Intelligence Analyst, Intelligence Operations Specialist
Graphic Design	Graphics Design, Visual Information Specialist, Multimedia Designer
Health Journalism	Writer-Editor, Public Affairs Specialist, Health Insurance Specialist
Health Services Research, Policy, and Administration.	Health Insurance Specialist, Health Information Specialist, Public Health Advisor, Public Health Analyst, Social Insurance Specialist (Claims Representative), Medical Records Administration Specialist
Hispanic Studies	Foreign Languages, International Broadcaster (Spanish)
History	Signals Analysis, Cryptanalyst, Intelligence Analyst, Program Analyst, Researcher, Archives Specialist
Human Resource Development	Human Resources, Equal Employment Opportunity Specialist, Management Specialist, Labor-Management Specialist
Industrial Engineering	Industrial Specialist, Occupational Safety and Health Specialist
Information Networking	Information Technology Specialist, Project Manager
Information Technology Infrastructure	Information Technology Specialist, Systems Analyst
International Business	Business Protocol Officer, Risk Analyst/Forecaster, Strategic Consultant, International Relations Specialist, International Economist, International Cooperative Program Specialist, Export Policy Analyst
International Relations	Center Adjudications Officer, Import Policy Analyst, International Activities Assistant, Research Analyst, Program Officer, Desk Officer, Regional Security Officer, Special Agent, Systems Analyst, Mediator
Japanese	Foreign Languages, Cryptanalyst, Intelligence Specialist, Passport Officer
Journalism	Writer-Editor, Public Affairs Specialist, Program & Management Analyst
Latin	Foreign Languages, Intelligence Operations Specialist
Law	Attorney-Advisor, Staff Attorney, Paralegal Specialist, Administrative Investigator, Policy Analyst
Legal Studies	Paralegal Specialist, Management Specialist
Liberal Studies	Community Outreach Specialist, Intelligence Operations Specialist, Industrial Security Specialist
Library Science	Librarian, Archivist, Media Specialist, Archives Specialist
Linguistics	Signals Analysis, Cryptanalyst, Intelligence Analyst
Management Information Systems	Information Technology Specialist
Management of Technology	Information Technology Specialist, Program Analyst
Manufacturing Technology	Quality Assurance Specialist, Production Management, Industrial Security Specialist

Find Your Federal Job Chart

MAJOR	FEDERAL JOB TITLES
Marketing	Contract Specialist, Purchasing Agent, Business & Industry Specialist, Consumer Affairs Specialist
Marketing and Logistics Management	Logistics Management Specialist, General Supply Specialist, Transportation Specialist
Mass Communication	Writer-Editor, Public Information Specialist, Audio-Visual Specialist
Materials Science and Engineering	Materials Management Specialist, Fire Management Officer
Mathematics	Signals Analysis, Cryptanalyst, Intelligence Analyst, Quality Assurance Specialist, Statistician, Mathemetician
Mechanical Engineering	Mechanical Engineer
Microbiology, Immunology, and Cancer Biology	Microbiologist, Biologist
Molecular Biology	Molecular Biology, Health Scientist
Molecular, Cellular, Developmental Biology, and Genetics	Geneticist
Multimedia	Multimedia Specialist, Visual Information Specialist, Audio-Visual Specialist
Natural Resources and Environmental Studies	Natural Conservation Resource Specialist, Environmental Protection Specialist
Network Administration	Information Technology Specialist, Systems Analyst
Nursing	Nurse, Health Insurance Specialist, Psychiatric Nurse, Surgical Technician
Operations and Management Science	Production Manager, Program Manager, Disaster Recovery & Operations Specialist
Pharmaceutics	Researcher, Pharmacist
Philosophy	Intelligence Operations Specialist, Ethics Program Specialist
Physical Education and Recreation	Morale, Recreation & Welfare Counselor, Fitness Instruction, Recreation Planner
Physics	Physics, Health Physicist, Occupational Safety and Health Specialist
Planning—See Urban and Regional Planning	Realty Specialist, Housing Management Specialist
Plant Biology	Botanist, Plant Pathologist, Plant Physiologist
Political Science	Policy Analyst, Congressional Affairs Specialist, Legislative Analyst, Transformation Facilitator
Psychology	Victim Specialist, Grant Program Specialist, Transformation Facilitator
Public Affairs	Public Affairs Specialist, Community Outreach Specialist
Public Health Administration	Health Systems Specialist, Health Information Specialist
Public Policy	Public Policy Analyst, International Trade Compliance Analyst, International Relations Specialist, Speechwriter, Foreign Service Officer

MAJOR	FEDERAL JOB TITLES
Rehabilitation Science	Rehabilitation Specialist, Fitness Specialist
Retail Merchandising	Supply Analyst, Purchase Agent, Contract Specialist
Rhetoric and Scientific and Technical Communication	Cryptanalyst, Intelligence Specialist
Risk Management and Insurance	Program Analyst, Source Management Officer, Loan Specialist (Realty)
Russian	Foreign Languages, Intelligence Analyst, Cryptanalyst, Foreign Service Officer
Science in Agriculture	Agronomist, Agriculture Extension
Science, Technology, and Environmental Policy	Environmental Protection Specialist, Program Analyst
Scientific and Technical Communication	Technical Writer, Writer-Editor, Policy Analyst
Social Work	Social Worker, Social Psychologist, Program Analyst, Management Analyst
Sociology	Victim Specialist, Grant Program Specialist
Software Engineering	Information Technology Specialist, Computer Scientist
Soil Science	Agronomist, Agriculture Extension, Entomologist, Soil Conservation, Soil Scientist
Spanish	Foreign Language, Center Adjudications Officer, Immigration Specialist
Special Education—See Educational Psychology	Education Specialist
Speech and Hearing Science	Researcher
Statistics	Mathematical Statistician, Statistician, Quality Assurance Specialist, Operations Research Analyst, Economic Research Analyst
Strategic Management and Organization—See Business Administration	Program Analyst, Management Analyst
Supply Chain Management	Supply Analyst, Logistics Management Specialist
Toxicology	Toxicologist, Chemist
Transportation	Program Specialist, Logistics Management Specialist
Urban and Community Forestry	Sylviculturist, Environmental Protection Specialist
Urban and Regional Planning	Natural Conservation Resource Specialist, Environmental Protection Specialist
Veterinary Medicine	Veterinarian
Water Resources Science	Natural Conservation Resource Specialist, Environmental Protection Specialist
Wildlife Conservation	Wildlife Biologist, Animal Scientist

Federal Classification and Job Grading System

All federal jobs are grouped into series that are given a numerical code for identification. Often positions that interest you may fall within several different series, while at other times, your positions of interest may only be located in one occupational group. It is a good idea to be familiar with these series numbers, or what the government calls the "Federal Classification and Job Grading System." The Office of Personnel Management has all the job classifications on their website at *www.opm.gov/fedclass/html/gsseries.asp*. As you can see, there are 23 Occupational Groups:

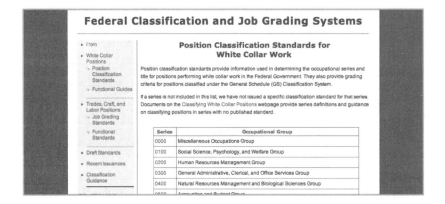

www.opm.gov/fedclass/html/gsseries.asp

Within each Occupational Group are several Occupation Series, as you can see from the 300 group below:

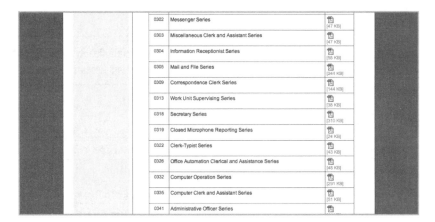

All of these occupations are described in great detail and will give you a clearer understanding of what these positions do. You can also use these descriptions to identify keywords for both your USAJOBS searches and for your federal resume.

How to Find Your Grade Level

The federal government determines your eligibility for a job at a certain grade level and salary by assessing your education and experience. For many occupations, experience is paramount, but education can be substituted for experience up to GS-11.

Educational Qualifications Chart

Qualifying Based on Education Alone	
GS-2	High school graduation or equivalent (i.e., GED)
GS-3	One year above high school
GS-4	Two years above high school (or Associate's Degree)
GS-5	Four years above high school leading to a Bachelor's Degree or a Bachelor's Degree
GS-7	One full year of graduate study or Bachelor's degree with Superior Academic Achievement (SAA) (See the table below for more information on SAA)
GS-9	Master's Degree or equivalent (e.g., J.D. or LL.B.) or two years of graduate education
GS-11	Ph.D. or three years of graduate school For research positions only: completion of all requirements for Master's Degree
GS-12	For research positions only: completion of all requirements for a doctoral or equivalent degree
Note: All positions at or above GS-13 require appropriate specialized experience, and do not allow education to be substituted for that specialized experience.	

Superior Academic Achievement and Grade Adjustments

The three ways to qualify for Superior Academic Achievement designation (and thus be eligible for GS-7 with only a Baccalaureate degree)		
1.	Class standing	Must be in the upper third of your graduating class in your college, university, or major subdivision such as the School of Business.
2.	Grade-point average (GPA)*	a. 3.0 out of a possible 4.0 ("B" or better) recorded on your transcript, or as computed based on 4 years of education, or as computed based on all courses completed during the final 2 years of your curriculum, or b. 3.5 or higher out of a possible 4.0 ("B+" or better) based on the average of the required courses completed in the major field or the required courses in the major field completed during the final 2 years of the curriculum.
3.	Election to membership in a National Honor Society	Honor societies listed in the Association of College Honor Society of American College Fraternities (1991) meet this requirement. Membership in a freshman honor society does not meet this requirement.
* OPM instructions say GPA should be credited in the manner most beneficial to the applicant.		

Federal Grade and Pay Structure

The federal civil service has different grading and pay structures for its professional and trade workforces. Because you are most likely a college student or graduate, we're going to focus on professional jobs ranging from accountants and cryptanalysts to special agents and biologists. The government categorizes this broad group of job titles in a system called PATCO, which stands for Professional, Administrative, Clerical, Technical, and Other.

PATCO Guide

Federal jobs are made up of the following basic categories, titles, and grades:

PROFESSIONAL – GS-5 through 15

These professional positions have a POSITIVE EDUCATIONAL REQUIREMENT, including such occupations as chemist, accountant, doctor, engineer, social worker, or psychologist. Where there is an educational requirement, the education must meet standards set by the profession involved.

ADMINISTRATIVE – GS-5 through 15

These jobs usually have the title of ANALYST or SPECIALIST. You can qualify for these jobs solely on the basis of experience, but below GS-12 education can be substituted for the required experience. If you have no experience, then you need a degree to qualify for entry-level (GS-5 and 7) administrative positions. Certain law enforcement investigative and inspection positions are in this category (e.g., Special Agent, Border Patrol, Customs Inspector, Immigration Inspector).

TECHNICAL – GS-6 through 9

These jobs are the TECHNICIAN or ASSISTANT positions, such as Accounting Technician or Assistant. Although a two or four-year degree may be required in some fields (especially medical technician occupations), the primary qualifications requirement is experience. Bachelor's degree graduates can qualify for Technician or Assistant positions starting at GS-7 with superior academic achievement.

CLERICAL – GS-1 through 5

These are the clerical positions. There is no college degree requirement. An Associate of Arts degree or two-year certification program will qualify for GS-3 or 4 positions.

OTHER

This category includes jobs that do not fit other categories. It includes many law enforcement occupations, including security guard, police, ranger, park ranger, and U.S. Marshal but does not include criminal investigators ("special agents"). Research psychologists and social scientists are also among the occupations in this category. The grades for this "Other" category can range from GS-3 to GS-15.

The GS Pay System

Professional jobs are organized into one of 15 grades in a system called the General Schedule. General Schedule grades represent levels of difficulty and responsibility that are in fact defined by law. They are identified by the letters "GS" followed by numbers, such as GS-1 (the lowest grade) to GS- 15 (the highest). A recent graduate with a bachelor's degree would usually qualify for a GS-5 or 7.

Salary Table 2013-GS*

Rates Frozen at 2010 Levels
Effective January 2013
Annual Rates by Grade and Step

Grade	Step 1	Step 2	Step 3	Step 4	Step 5	Step 6	Step 7	Step 8	Step 9	Step 10	WGI
1	17,803	18,398	18,990	19,579	20,171	20,519	21,104	21,694	21,717	22,269	552
2	20,017	20,493	21,155	21,717	21,961	22,607	23,253	23,899	24,545	25,191	646
3	21,840	22,568	23,296	24,024	24,752	25,480	26,208	26,936	27,664	28,392	728
4	24,518	25,335	26152	26,969	27,786	28,603	29,420	30,237	31,054	31,871	817
5	27,431	28,345	29,259	30,173	31,087	32,001	32,915	33,829	34,743	35,657	914
6	30,577	31,596	32,615	33,634	34,653	35,672	36,691	37,710	38,729	39,748	1,019
7	33,979	35,112	36,245	37,378	38,511	39,644	40,777	41,910	43,043	44,176	1,133
8	37,631	38,885	40,139	41,393	42,647	43,901	45,155	46,409	47,663	48,917	1,254
9	41,563	42,948	44,333	45,718	47,103	48,488	49,873	51,258	52,643	54,028	1,385
10	45,771	47,297	48,823	50,349	51,875	53,401	54,927	56,453	57,979	59,505	1,526
11	50,287	51,963	53,639	55,315	56,991	58,667	60,343	62,019	63,695	65,371	1,676
12	60,274	62,283	64,292	66,301	68,310	70,319	72,328	74,337	76,346	78,355	2,009
13	71,674	74,063	76,452	78,841	81,230	83,619	86,008	88,397	90,786	93,175	2,389
14	84,697	87,520	90,343	93,166	95,989	98,812	101,635	104,458	107,281	110,104	2,823
15	99,628	102,949	106,270	109,591	112,912	116,233	119,554	122,875	126,196	129,517	3,321

*Salary rates based on location. Locality examples:

Grade and Step	Denver, CO	Milaukee, WI	Washington, DC
GS-5, Step 1	$33,608	$32,396	$34,075
GS-7, Step 1	$41,631	$40,129	$42,209
GS-9, Step 1	$50,923	$49,086	$51,630
GS-11, Step 1	$61,612	$59,389	$62,467

When Veterans Preference Does Not Apply

Veterans preference basically means that, for many jobs, certain veteran candidates must be hired unless HR can make a reasonable justification not to do so. There is one exception, and that is for Scientific and Professional positions at the GS-9 level or higher. A list of the occupational series covered by this qualification standard is provided below. More information about Scientific and Professional positions can be found at https://www.opm.gov/policy-data-oversight/classification-qualifications/general-schedule-qualification-standards/#url=GS-PROF

GS-020 Community Planning
GS-101 Social Science
GS-110 Economist
GS-130 Foreign Affairs
GS-131 International Relations
GS-140 Workforce Research and Analysis
GS-150 Geography
GS-170 History
GS-180 Psychology
GS-184 Sociology
GS-185 Social Work
GS-190 General Anthropology
GS-193 Archeology
GS-401 General Biological Science
GS-403 Microbiology
GS-405 Pharmacology
GS-408 Ecology
GS-410 Zoology
GS-413 Physiology
GS-414 Entomology
GS-415 Toxicology
GS-430 Botany
GS-434 Plant Pathology
GS-435 Plant Physiology
GS-436 Plant Protection and Quarantine
GS-437 Horticulture
GS-440 Genetics
GS-454 Rangeland Management
GS-457 Soil Conservation
GS-460 Forestry
GS-470 Soil Science
GS-471 Agronomy
GS-480 General Fish and Wildlife Administration
GS-482 Fishery Biology
GS-485 Wildlife Refuge Management
GS-486 Wildlife Biology
GS-487 Animal Science

GS-510 Accounting
GS-511 Auditing
GS-512 Internal Revenue Agent
GS-601 General Health Science
GS-630 Dietitian and Nutritionist
GS-631 Occupational Therapist
GS-633 Physical Therapist
GS-635 Corrective Therapist
GS-637 Manual Arts Therapist
GS-638 Recreation/Creative Arts Therapist
GS-639 Educational Therapist
GS-644 Medical Technologist
GS-665 Speech Pathology and Audiology
GS-690 Industrial Hygiene
GS-696 Consumer Safety
GS-801 General Engineering
GS-803 Safety Engineering
GS-804 Fire Protection Engineering
GS-806 Materials Engineering
GS-807 Landscape Architecture
GS-808 Architecture
GS-810 Civil Engineering
GS-819 Environmental Engineering
GS-830 Mechanical Engineering
GS-840 Nuclear Engineering
GS-850 Electrical Engineering
GS-854 Computer Engineering
GS-855 Electronics Engineering
GS-858 Biomedical Engineering
GS-861 Aerospace Engineering
GS-871 Naval Architecture
GS-880 Mining Engineering
GS-881 Petroleum Engineering
GS-890 Agricultural Engineering
GS-892 Ceramic Engineering
GS-893 Chemical Engineering
GS-894 Welding Engineering
GS-896 Industrial Engineering
GS-1015 Museum Curator

GS-1221 Patent Adviser
GS-1223 Patent Classifying
GS-1224 Patent Examining
GS-1226 Design Patent Examining
GS-1301 General Physical Science
GS-1306 Health Physics
GS-1310 Physics
GS-1313 Geophysics
GS-1315 Hydrology
GS-1320 Chemistry
GS-1321 Metallurgy
GS-1330 Astronomy and Space Science
GS-1340 Meteorology
GS-1350 Geology
GS-1360 Oceanography
GS-1370 Cartography
GS-1372 Geodesy
GS-1373 Land Surveying
GS-1380 Forest Products Technology
GS-1382 Food Technology
GS-1384 Textile Technology
GS-1386 Photographic Technology
GS-1420 Archivist
GS-1510 Actuary
GS-1515 Operations Research
GS-1520 Mathematics
GS-1529 Mathematical Statistician
GS-1530 Statistician
GS-1550 Computer Science
GS-1701 General Education and Training
GS-1710 Education and Vocational Training
GS-1720 Education Program
GS-1725 Public Health Educator
GS-1730 Education Research
GS-1740 Education Services
GS-1750 Instructional Systems

STEP 4: Search USAJOBS for Pathways Announcements

Additional Student Veterans info on page 91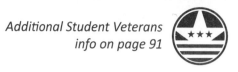

Search Strategies for Finding Student Positions and Employment Opportunities

This step will help you find and interpret vacancy announcements both for student opportunities and for full-time positions through the competitive hiring process. Therefore, this step is divided into three sections:

⇢ Aspects that relate to both student and employment opportunities
⇢ Finding and applying to student or recent graduate programs
⇢ Finding and applying to federal job announcements

SAMPLE PATHWAYS ANNOUNCEMENT

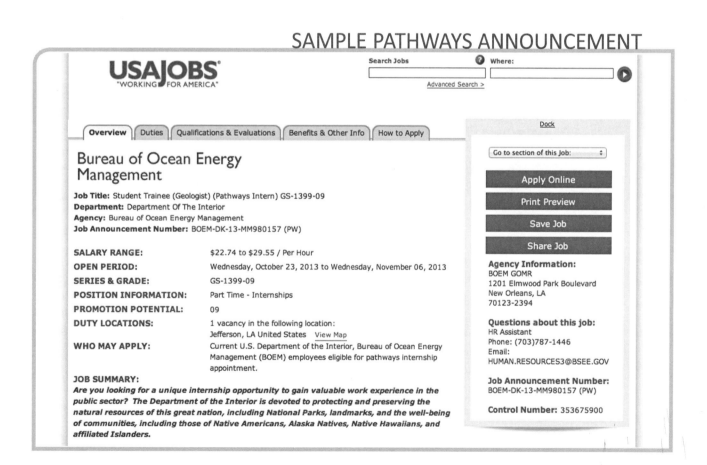

Federal Job Search Tips for Students

How are student programs and employment opportunities the same?
There are several aspects to searching for student opportunities and employment positions that are similar. In fact, the following points are usually true for your career searches in general.

Start your search early
We all know those people who seem to be at the right place at the right time . . . all the time. Odds are those people spend time preparing and researching well in advance. Therefore, it is never too early to start your search for a rewarding internship or job—and it is never too late, either. Even if you are just starting your undergraduate program and do not want to do a federal internship for two more summers, you can start researching those agencies and programs that interest you the most. The earlier you start this process, the greater your knowledge of yourself and the government, and the larger your network.

Apply to those agencies with missions that appeal to you
By starting early, doing your research, and asking questions of the experts in your network, you learn more about an agency than you would simply by applying to a position. That knowledge will help you identify places, people, and environments that appeal to you the most, which is very important. It is a good idea to focus on the positions that most appeal to you, because that is where you will find the most opportunities to grow and learn.

Apply to positions with job duties and in locations that fit you
Everyone has had jobs they couldn't stand, and we all want to avoid them at all costs. Many times, unfortunately, people apply for positions that do not fit their interests for several good reasons, not the least of which is economic need. The more a position is of interest to you, the more likely you will enjoy what you do and subsequently grow and develop professionally. Keep in mind too, the more flexible you are with location, the better your chances of being hired.

Apply to positions you that match your qualifications
There are so many terrific opportunities in the federal government that it is tempting to apply to as many as possible. Before you do that, make sure you meet the qualifications of every position so you do not waste your time. Applying to every federal opportunity is time consuming for you and for those reviewing applications. Take the time to honestly assess your fit for each position, and when you aren't sure, contact your network for help.

Identify keywords and read the entire vacancy announcement
As you will see over and over in the rest of this book, successful applicants (students or otherwise) know what the employer wants. That means identifying and using keywords from the position announcements as much as possible. Therefore, you MUST read the entire announcement to make sure you address all of THEIR needs.

Finding Student and Recent Graduate Opportunities

As you saw in Step 3, there are many great student and recent graduate positions available throughout the United States. With the implementation of the Pathways Programs, most opportunities can now be found on USAJOBS. You can start with the Student section of USAJOBS at *www.usajobs.gov/StudentsandGrads*.

You can also look for opportunities on the websites of the agencies that interest you the most. There are far too many agencies for you to cover, which is why it is very important that you focus on those places that interest you the most.

Below is an example of the Federal Emergency Management Agency's US National Fire Administration Internship Program. This is an internship for students interested in in fire service and emergency management.

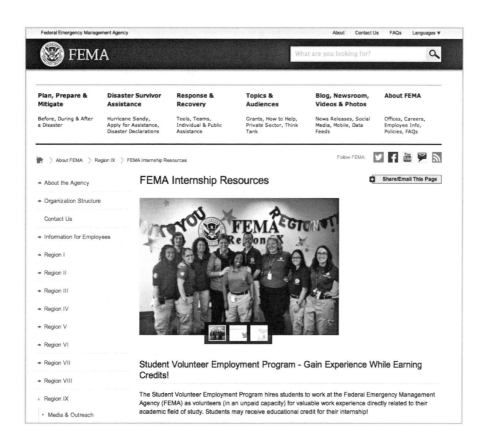

www.fema.gov/fema-internship-resources-0

www.usfa.fema.gov/about/jobs/internship.shtm

Your personal network of fellow students, alumni, faculty, and other professionals is a great place to find out about opportunities not otherwise posted publicly. One of the best resources you have to identify positions and to build your network is your college's or university's career services center (as a student and as an alum). Many career services centers will be happy to help alumni as well as students, and often they do it for free. Therefore, get in touch with them sooner rather than later so your alma mater can continue to help you.

Note about U.S. citizenship:

As a general rule, only U.S. citizens or nationals are eligible for student programs and employment in the civil service. In addition, Congress annually imposes a ban on using appropriated funds to hire noncitizens within the United States (certain groups of noncitizens are not included in this ban). Further, immigration law limits public and private sector hiring to only individuals who are 1) U.S. citizens or nationals; 2) aliens assigned by the U.S. Citizenship and Immigration Services (CIS) to a class of immigrants authorized to be employed (the largest group in this class is aliens lawfully admitted for permanent U.S. residence); or 3) an individual alien expressly authorized by the CIS to be employed.

Despite all of these limitations and restrictions, it is possible for noncitizens to be hired into student programs or employment positions. For example, an agency may hire a qualified noncitizen in the excepted service or the Senior Executive Service if it is permitted to do so by the annual appropriations act and immigration law. If agencies cannot find qualified citizens to fill jobs in the competitive service, they may then hire noncitizens for those jobs. However, noncitizens may only be given an excepted appointment and will never acquire "status." They may not be promoted or reassigned to another civil service job except in situations where qualified citizens are not available.

USAJOBS Search Strategies

Most federal government positions are posted to USAJOBS. There are an average of 5,000 jobs listed on the site on any given day. There are also a number of Excepted Agencies that do not need to post their jobs on USAJOBS. Often these agencies will post some of their vacancies on USAJOBS, but many more can be found either on their individual websites or on other sites such as AvueCentral.

With all of the positions posted to USAJOBS, how do you find the right position for you? We'll show you some ways to refine your search.

Create Your USAJOBS Profile
Log in and then go to My Account > Profile.

USAJOBS Profile Page

Search on the keyword "Pathways"
From the home page or the advanced search page, try to do a search on the keyword "Pathways". This search will tell you how many Pathways internships are currently available and what types of internships are out there now.

USAJOBS Advanced Search Page

Refine Your Search

It is a good idea to start searching broadly to catch as many positions related to your interests as possible. However, looking through lists of hundreds of positions can be frustrating and tiring. As you gain a better understanding of what works best for you, use the Advanced Search section (left). On this page you can search using any or all of the following criteria:

Keywords

Keywords can be words, phrases, job numbers, series numbers, and terms you use to describe educational and professional experiences, skills, and agency names. This is the broadest way to search for positions, but it is often hard to match your description of a position with the federal government's description. USAJOBS gives you instructions on how to maximize your keyword search, too.

Title Search

It is important to search for ALL JOBS because federal job titles are not as straightforward as we would like, and they are prone to change as new job needs arise in agencies. If you limit your job search to a particular job title with which you are familiar, you may not learn about all of the job openings for which you are qualified or even those that represent your particular field of interest. For instance, would you automatically think to search for Program Specialist or Management Analyst? Surprisingly, these popular government job titles mean many things. The range of program possibilities is phenomenal—environment, food and nutrition, transportation, education, health, health insurance, homeland security. You name it, the government probably has a program specialist or management analyst working on it!

Series Number Search

Identify the series number for the job titles that interest you (more information about the "Federal Classifications and Job Grading System" in Step 3). Type in these numbers to search for the job titles. For example, search on "0303" for administrative support assistant.

Location Search

This allows you to specify where you would like to work. Again, it is best to be very broad when using this search. Unless you know of a position that is in a very specific location, you do not want to miss opportunities that could be located nearby but listed differently in this search field.

Agency Search

This is another field that is best used when you have a specific position in mind. There are so many great opportunities in the federal government that you may miss an analyst position at the National Nuclear Security Administration (NNSA) that fits your interests if you look solely in the Department of State.

Salary Range or Pay Grade (GS) Search

The actual salary that an agency offers will be dependent on your qualifications. It is very difficult to know for which salary ranges you qualify. Pay Grades will be discussed more in Step 5, and you can find a list of salary ranges online at *www.opm.gov/flsa/oca/11tables/*. For now, you can follow these general guidelines:

> › If you are a BA/BS graduate, then you should search at GS-5 to 7 ($27,400-$44,100)
> › If you are an advanced degree graduate or have one year of specialized experience, you can begin your search at GS-9 ($41,500-$54,000)
> › If you are a two-year college graduate or technical training school graduate, then you would search for jobs at the GS-3 to 4 range based on your training ($21,800-$31,800)
> › If you are a high school student, you can search for student jobs at the grade levels GS-2 and 3 ($20,000-$28,300)
> *(See the Educational Qualifications Chart on page 97)*

Eligibility Search

Much like private sector companies and nonprofits, the federal government likes to hire from within. That means only those who are current or former federal employees are eligible to apply. If you have never worked for the federal government, you should choose "No" in this box to avoid seeing those positions for which you are not eligible.

Save Your Search

You can save the searches to automaticlaly bring up the most interesting positions for you.

Create automatic email alerts in USAJOBS to receive notification when job openings are posted relating to your search.

Sample Pathways Announcements (October 24, 2013)

AGENCY NAME	TYPE	TITLE	GRADE LEVELS	MAJORS DESIRED
National Aeronautics and Space Administration (NASA)	Internship	Emergency Management	GS-0099-7/11	Emergency Management, Homeland Security, Intelligence Studies, Public Administration
NASA	Recent Graduate	Aerospace Technologist (AST), Flight Systems Training and Operations	GS-0801-9	Electrical Engineering, Computer Engineering, Mechanical Engineering, Aerospace Engineering, Physics
Consumer Financial Protection Bureau (CFPB)	Recent Graduate	CFPB Pathways Recent Graduate	CN-22/51 ($29,735 to $93,380)	Various Business, Management, Financial Positions
U.S. Army Corps of Engineers (USACE)	Internship	Contracting	GS-1199-03/05	Accounting, Business Finance, Law, Contracts, Purchasing, Economics, Industrial Management, Marketing, Quantitative Methods, or Organization And Management
Bureau of Ocean Energy Management (BOEM)	Internship	Geologist	GS-1399-09	None specified (Duties: interpreting geological and geophysical data)
U.S. General Services Administration (GSA)	Recent Graduate	Realty Specialist	GS-1170-09	None specified (Duties: property acquisition and disposal)
National Park Service (NPS)	Internship	Park Ranger-Protection	GS-0099-05	Natural Resource Management, Natural Sciences, Earth Sciences, History, Archeology, Anthropology, Park and Recreation Management, Law Enforcement/Police Science, Social Sciences, Museum Sciences, Business Administration, Public Administration, Behavioral Sciences, Sociology, or other closely related subjects pertinent to the management and protection of natural and cultural resources
U.S. Army Corps of Engineers (USACE)	Internship	Social Sciences	GS-0190-5/7	Appropriate social science field such as Anthropology, Archeology, Geography, and/or Economics, etc.
National Institutes of Standards and Technology (NIST)	Internship	Physical Science Technician	ZT-1399-01 ($22,115 to $39,590)	None specified (Duties: general laboratory maintenance in a class 100 cleanroom)
National Credit Union Administration (NCUA)	Recent Graduate	Credit Union Examiner	CU-0580-07/09	Economics, Accounting, Business, Business Administration, Finance, Marketing, or other directly related business field
Veterans Affairs (VA)	Internship	Medical & Health	GS-0699-07/09	Masters degree program in Healthcare Administration
Patent and Trademark Office (PTO)	Internship	Patent Examiner	GS-1299-04	Computer Science, or a combination of Mathematics, Statistics, and computer Science
National Park Service (NPS)	Recent Graduate	Archeological Technician	GS-0102-05	Anthropology, Archeology

Excepted Service Agencies

Excepted Service agencies may or may not post their vacancy announcements on USAJOBS. You may need to check the websites of these agencies to find their job postings.

Executive Branch Agencies and Independent Departments:
→ Transportation Security Agency (TSA), Department of Homeland Security (DHS)
→ Federal Reserve System, Board of Governors
→ Central Intelligence Agency (CIA)
→ Defense Intelligence Agency (DIA), Department of Defense (DoD)
→ Foreign Service, Department of State (DoS)
→ Federal Bureau of Investigation (FBI), Department of Justice (DoJ)
→ National Security Agency (NSA), Department of Defense (DoD)
→ National Geospatial-Intelligence Agency (NGA), Department of Defense (DoD)
→ U.S. Nuclear Regulatory Commission (NRC)
→ Postal Rate Commission
→ Peace Corps
→ Health Services and Research Administration, Department of Veterans Affairs (physicians, nurses, and allied medical personnel)

Government Corporations, such as:
→ General Services Administration (GSA)
→ U.S. Postal Service
→ Tennessee Valley Authority
→ The Virgin Islands Corporation

Judicial Branch, such as:
→ Administrative Office of the U.S. Courts
→ U.S. Sentencing Commission

Legislative Branch, such as:
→ Government Accountability Office (GAO)
→ Library of Congress (including the Congressional Research Service)

STEP 5: Analyze Vacancy Announcements

Additional Student Veterans info on page 91

Strategies for Understanding USAJOBS Vacancy Announcements

→ Learn how to read vacancy announcements effectively and what to look for
→ Find keywords for your resume
→ Understand the definitions for applicant eligibility

SAMPLE PATHWAYS ANNOUNCEMENT

USAJOBS "WORKING FOR AMERICA"

Search Jobs   Where:
Advanced Search >

Overview | Duties | Qualifications & Evaluations | Benefits & Other Info | How to Apply

GSA U.S. General Services Administration

Job Title: Realty Specialist - Pathways Recent Graduates
Department: General Services Administration
Agency: Public Buildings Service
Job Announcement Number: 1307079DMOTR

SALARY RANGE:	$50,154.00 to $65,196.00 / Per Year
OPEN PERIOD:	Friday, October 18, 2013 to Friday, November 01, 2013
SERIES & GRADE:	GS-1170-09
POSITION INFORMATION:	Full-time - Excepted appointment which may be non-competitively converted to a term or permanent position.
PROMOTION POTENTIAL:	12
DUTY LOCATIONS:	FEW vacancies in the following location: Fort Worth, TX, US View Map
WHO MAY APPLY:	1. Graduates receiving a qualifying associates, bachelors, masters, professional, doctorate, vocational or technical degree or certificate from a qualifying educational institution within the past 2 years or after 12/27/2010. 2. Preference eligible veterans precluded from applying due to military service obligation may apply up to 2 years from the date of discharge/release from active duty, but no more than 6 years after the date educational requirements are met.

JOB SUMMARY:
You may have heard GSA called 'the government's landlord', but GSA is about more than just buildings...We're a vehicle management and acquisition service...a real estate manager...an IT solutions provider...a global supply chain manager...and more! GSA provides innovative solutions for Federal agencies that include products, services, workspace, and expertise to build a more high-performing, efficient, sustainable, and transparent government for the American people. And, since our jobs are as diverse as the services we provide, GSA is a great place to start, build, and expand your career.

Dock

Go to section of this Job:

Apply Online

Print Preview

Save Job

Share Job

Agency Information:
GSA, Public Buildings Service
General Services Administration
Human Resources Division (CPI)
819 Taylor St.
Fort Worth, TX
76102
US
Fax: 000-000-0000

Questions about this job:
Dolly Moreno
Phone: 817-978-2460
Fax: 000-000-0000
Email: vacancy.inquiries@gsa.gov

Job Announcement Number:
1307079DMOTR

Control Number: 353486300

How to Read Announcements

As you read the vacancy announcements in search of the perfect job opening, there are a few key points to remember:

1. Read the Instructions Very Carefully

ALL of the instructions must be followed exactly, or your application will be rejected. If you have any questions about the instructions, email or call the contact person listed in the announcement.

2. Specialized Experience

Your resume must demonstrate that you have the required One Year Specialized experience. If you cannot meet this qualification, then you need not apply.

3. Keywords

Keywords for your resume can be found in the following sections: duties, qualifications required, and the self-assessment questionnaire.

4. Preview the Self-Assessment Questionnaire

Take a peek at the self-assessment questionnaire to get a better idea of the qualifications they are looking for and to get an idea of how long it will take you to complete this portion of the application.

Specialized Experience is the GOLD in the vacancy announcement. Be sure to add your One Year of Qualifications to your federal resume.

Vacancy Announcement Sections Explained

Below are some more details about a few of the important announcement sections.

Series and Grade

If only one grade is listed, such as "GS-0101-12/12," this tells you that the agency is recruiting at only the GS-12 level. For the position below with the Department of the Interior, the Series and Grade is listed as "GS-0544-04/05," which means you can apply for this position at the GS-4 or GS-5 levels, or you can submit separate applications for both GS levels.

U.S. DEPARTMENT OF THE INTERIOR
Office of the Secretary

Job Title: Civilian Pay Clerk/Technician (Benefits)
Department: Department Of The Interior
Agency: Office of the Secretary of the Interior
Job Announcement Number: WHRMO519678JS

SALARY RANGE:	$30,039.00 - $43,687.00 /year
OPEN PERIOD:	Monday, August 15, 2011 to Friday, August 26, 2011
SERIES & GRADE:	GS-0544-04/05
POSITION INFORMATION:	Full Time Career/Career Conditional
PROMOTION POTENTIAL:	06
DUTY LOCATIONS:	1 vacancy - Denver, CO
WHO MAY BE CONSIDERED:	United States Citizens

JOB SUMMARY:
Join the Department of Interior's National Business Center!

Duties

Always read the duties carefully because the title of the position may not accurately reflect the duties of the job. The duties could represent a completely different job than the one you thought would be described. Sometimes government job titles just do not match the duties you would expect.

This is also where you will find many of the keywords you will need to use in your application to be successful.

Who May Be Considered

As with most companies and organizations, the federal government often has positions open only to current or recent employees. This type of eligibility is often referred to as "Status" or being "In Status." Several student programs will give you "Status" after you complete them, which is a major advantage for you. Also, another great perk of being a federal employee is that you can be granted permanent "tenure," or permanent "status," after you complete at least three years as a federal employee—and they do not need to be three years in a row.

Agencies will often list the same position twice: once for "status" applicants and once for any citizen who meets the qualifications. Make sure you are applying to the right position! And remember that "status" applicants can apply to positions open to all those who are qualified. In fact, they will have a leg up on those who are not status candidates.

Definitions of those who can apply include the following:

⇢ **Status Candidates:** Current federal employees in permanent positions, those within a year of leaving their federal position (e.g., returned Peace Corps volunteers and some student positions), or those federal employees who have "tenure" (federal employees for at least three years).

⇢ **Public:** Any interested U.S. citizen.

⇢ **U.S. Citizens:** Those who are U.S. citizens by birth or naturalization. Depending on the agency and the position, dual citizenship will work, but ask the HR professional. More information about U.S. Citizenship on page 44.

⇢ **Agency Employees Only:** Only those currently working at that particular department.

⇢ **All Groups of Qualified Individuals:** Everyone who meets the job requirements.

⇢ **Career Transition Assistance Program (CTAP):** Those federal employees being downsized who were given special preference to find another position in their agency.

⇢ **Interagency Career Transition Assistance Program (ICTAP):** Those federal employees being downsized who were given special preference to find another federal position at any agency that is not downsizing their type of position.

NOTE: Most federal civil service jobs require U.S. citizenship, but jobs in other federal systems (such as the Postal Service, National Institutes of Health, and other agencies) may not. If you are not a U.S. citizen, read this part of the announcement carefully.

Qualifications Required

Read the required qualifications to determine if you have the generalized and specialized experience or education that can substitute for it. This is another great area to find the important keywords HR professionals are looking for.

Key Tips:

→ "One year" means 52 weeks, 40 hours per week (excluding holidays, of course). Relevant experience gained from part-time jobs can be combined to determine how much job-related experience you have. If the hours combine to make one year of specialized experience, then you can be credited with that year.

→ For many jobs, qualifcations are expressed in terms of experience or education, or combinations of the two. Possession of a Bachelor's Degree is ofen enough to qualify someone for an entry-level (GS-5 or sometimes GS-7) job in many professional or administrative occupations—the type of jobs most graduates seek following college

→ For career changers returning to college for another degree, you may qualify for your new career as a GS-5, 7, or 9 based on your education alone. You will probably have to take a step back in expected earnings, but you can move ahead in your new career

Many agencies use self-assessment questionnaires to rate and rank applicants. These questions give you another source of keywords and they can help you determine if, given your qualifications, you should apply to the position at hand. Below right is part of a sample questionnaire.

For this position, there are 22 questions to answer, all of which give you more information on the position and what you must include in your application. Question 3 wants to know how well you communicate technical and non-technical information in writing, while question 4 asks about how well you work with other mental health providers. Obviously, then, these are two very important aspects to the position, which may not have been communicated clearly in the Duties section.

YOUR RESPONSES TO THE FOLLOWING QUESTIONS MUST BE SUPPORTED IN YOUR RESUME. FAILURE TO SUPPORT YOUR ANSWER(S) IN YOUR RESUME MAY IMPACT YOU OR ELIMINATE YOU FROM CONSIDERATION.

* 3.From the answer choices below, please select the one that best reflects your ability to communicate technical and non-technical information in writing:

1. I have experience writing only non-technical information for my peers.

2. I have experience writing only technical information for my peers.

3. I have experience writing both technical and non-technical information for peers.

4. I have written both technical and non-technical types of information on the job for superiors, co-workers, consumers and others. I am proficient at this job function.

5. I have been acknowledged for my ability to write technical and non-technical information for a variety of inside and outside readers. My writing skills are considered to be of superior quality.

6. None of the above.

* 4.Have you developed and maintained an effective working relationship with local, State and Federal agencies and related mental health providers?

1. I have not had experience, education, or training in performing this task.

2. I have had education or training in performing this task but have not yet performed this task on the job.

3. I have performed this task on the job with close supervision from supervisor or senior employee.

4. I have performed this task as a regular part of the job, independently and usually without review by supervisor or senior employee.

5. I have supervised performance of this task, and/or I have trained others in performance and/or am normally consulted as an expert for assistance in performing this task.

STEP 6: Write Your Federal Resume

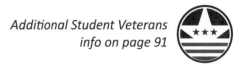

Additional Student Veterans info on page 91

How Can I Make My Resume Stand Out?

Your resume is the most important document you will write and submit for a federal job or internship. For either application, your federal resume is your federal application. You may be required to submit other documents, but the resume is your primary application. Of all the steps in the book, this one is the most important. If you apply to jobs for which you are qualified, the resume serves as your first impression and can make you stand out against your competition.

SAMPLE PATHWAYS ANNOUNCEMENT

Key Components of Your Federal Resume

Job Information
Announcement number, title and grade(s) of the position

Personal Information
- Full name, mailing address (with zip code) and day and evening phone numbers (with area code)
- Country of citizenship (most federal jobs require United States citizenship)
- Veterans' preference
- Reinstatement eligibility (if requested, attach SF-50 as proof of your career or career-conditional status)
- Highest federal civilian grade held (also give job series and dates held)

Education
- High school
- Name, city, state, zip (if known)
- Date of diploma or GED
- Colleges or universities
- Name, city, state, zip (if known)
- Major(s)
- Type and year of any degrees received (if no degree, show total credits earned and indicate whether semester or quarter hours)
- Send a copy of your college transcript only if the job vacancy announcement requests it

Work Experience
Give the following information for your paid and nonpaid work related to the job to which you are applying (do not send job descriptions):
- Job title (include series and grade if federal job)
- Duties and accomplishments
- Employer's name and address
- Supervisor's name and phone number
- Starting and ending dates (month and year)
- Hours per week
- Salary
- Indicate whether HR or hiring manager may contact your current supervisor

Other Qualifications
- JOB-RELATED training courses (title and year)
- JOB-RELATED skills (e.g., other languages, computer software/hardware, tools, machinery, typing speed)
- JOB-RELATED certificates and licenses (current only)
- JOB-RELATED honors, awards and special accomplishments, e.g., publications, memberships in professional or honor societies, leadership activities, public speaking, and performance awards (give dates but do not send documents unless requested)

Keywords Make Your Application Stand Out!

Every job and industry has its own specific language, and each federal resume needs to include the appropriate keywords. Federal HR professionals are inundated with recruitment duties and have hundreds of applications to process. If your application contains the best keywords drawn from the position announcement, you make their job easier! The way to stand out from other qualified applicants is by using the keywords and skills from the announcement.

Where can you find the federal keywords?

As discussed in Step 5, keywords can be found in vacancy announcements in several locations: Duties, Qualifications, Questionnaires, Job Questions, and sometimes in other paragraphs. Read the entire announcement for keywords to include in your resume.

The following announcement is filled with keywords, skills, and duties that should be addressed in the applicant's federal resume. The keywords are in bold.

U.S. Agency for International Development Agency

Position Title, Series, Grade: NEW ENTRY PROFESSIONAL PROGRAM, Contracting

Officer, FS-4; Salary: $41,379.00 - $74,994.00 Annual; Duty Location(s): Worldwide

Contracting Officers in USAID **plan, negotiate, award, and administer contracts, grants, and other agreements** with individuals, firms, and institutions to carry out USAID financed projects. Duties include providing **technical guidance and assistance** to USAID's overseas and Washington staffs, and host country officials in the **negotiation and awarding of contracts and grants.**

DUTIES:

Supports activities within the **contracting** sector by **reviewing and analyzing data; developing strategies, analytical models, and methodologies; and providing assistance and advice on contracting issues.**

Develops, oversees, manages, and evaluates contracting and assistance activities. **Plans** contracting and assistance activities such as **procurement analysis, contract negotiation, contract cost/price analysis, and policy review. Plans, negotiates, awards, and administers contracts, grants**, and other agreements with individuals, firms, and institutions to carry out **USAID-financed projects.**

KNOWLEDGE, SKILLS AND ABILITIES:

Knowledge of **contracting laws**, regulations, principles, policies, and procedures.

Ability to **manage and build teams.**

Ability to **communicate effectively** other than in writing.

Ability to communicate in **writing.**

Relevant majors are **business administration, public administration, law, banking, international affairs, procurement and contracting or finance with an emphasis on commerce, trade, and materials management.**

Relevant experience is defined as professional contracting or procurement work.

The following Summary of Skills includes the keywords and skills which were in bold from the previous announcement. This will be at the top of your federal resume.

SUMMARY OF SKILLS:

Contract Management — MBA coursework concentrated in contract management, including Federal Acquisition Regulations.

Customer Service and Technical Guidance for Contractor Support — Member of team providing customer service and technical support throughout system training and upgrades.

Developing Contracting Strategies — Strategic planning courses and projects demonstrate my ability to be resourceful and creative in researching, writing, and planning organizational strategies for business development and growth.

Team Leadership — Team leader with experience in planning projects, timelines, and objectives for six different teams engaged in major class projects during my college years. Skilled in delegating and reviewing project status and follow-up. Recognize the importance of communication to keep projects moving.

Writing Skill — Efficient researcher skilled in writing coursework, papers, and research projects.

Communication — Experienced in theater, speech, and debate and in making presentations throughout college.

How to Highlight Your Education

Since you are just completing your education, this section is CRITICAL for your federal job or internship application. Your courses, projects, research papers, and activities are likely to be what will impress the human resources staff and the hiring manager. If you don't have a degree yet, list the number of credit hours you have completed and whether they are semester or quarter hours.

You will primarily be using your education and academic experiences to become Best Qualified for your target position, so you will need to expand this information.

Relevant Courses and Descriptions

The vacancy announcement will list any courses that are required for the position. Be sure to list the relevant courses in your resume in addition to providing a copy of your transcript. The course description can be important for critical courses so that the HR staff will see the keywords, and the supervisor will understand courses that may not be clear without the description.

Academic Projects

Many courses include a project or research paper where you worked individually or as part of a team. Write about your major projects and papers. The HR reviewers will see keywords and skills that relate to the position. Because you are a recent or soon-to-be graduate, your most important experiences may be course projects and papers.

Academic Honors

This section may include scholarships, fellowships, the Dean's list, graduation with honors, honorary societies, letters of recognition, or ROTC military honors.

Academic Activities

Your academic activities demonstrate specialized interests, skills, and values. If you are a member of a sports team, you demonstrate discipline, teamwork, ability to manage a schedule, and dedication. If you are in theater or debate, you demonstrate communications skills, practice, teamwork, and again, dedication to a group effort (which will be important in your federal career). Federal jobs are performed in teams many times—groups of employees combine to implement programs and provide services to various customers. Activities also show that you can handle multiple projects and deadlines, and work with diverse groups.

Academic Papers and Publications

Writing articles, papers, presentations, speeches, and reports for courses, newspapers, and other print media can be very helpful for the KSA, "Ability to Communicate in Writing." Federal employees communicate in writing every day – via emails, briefings, researching and summarizing information, website content, memos, letters, and more. Writing is a critical skill in government, so include your writing experience from college.

Presentations

Depending on your major and degree, you may have had the opportunity to give presentations, speeches, and briefings. Make it clear in your resume that you have given presentations for courses, associations, or volunteer activities. "Ability to communicate other than in writing" is an important government skill. Federal employees talk and listen to customers, co-workers, other agencies, and contractors. You may negotiate, lead, or give briefings, using experience you gained in college.

Training, Workshops, and Conferences

Be sure to include special workshops, training programs, and conferences you may have attended during college. Specialized courses demonstrate that you have sought out additional training and networked within a particular field of work.

Certifications

Separate your certification programs from your courses and internships. If you are certified in First Aid, Lifeguard Training, CPR, SCUBA, computers, or other certifications, include these. Job-related certifications are impressive to HR staffing specialists, as well as the manager.

USAJOBS will allow you to save up to five different resumes in your account. Target your resumes to different occupational series, and name them carefully.

Work and Internship Experience

This is either the most or second most important section in your federal resume. That depends on your experience. Your paid and non-paid experience gained from jobs and internships is critical to how competitive your application is. One of the biggest challenges of writing your position descriptions is writing in some detail, including specific projects, knowledge gained, skills developed, and missions or programs supported.

Your application will be scored on a scale of up to 100. To be Best Qualified and have your resume forwarded to the hiring supervisor, your application must score 90 and above.

This section of the federal resume is different from a resume aimed at private industry. A federal resume should include sufficient information so that HR reviewers can check your references and determine how much time you spent performing specialized work during your work and internship experiences. Federal agencies may total up your hours spent doing a particular kind of specialized work to see if it amounts to a year or more. The agency then determines the level of the work experience. It is possible to qualify for a higher grade or salary than you initially expected because of part-time work and internship experiences. But you have to furnish the information if you want it to be considered. Include the following information for each position that is relevant to your career objective:

Job Title

Workplace Name, Address, State, Zip

Ending Salary

Hours Per Week

Supervisor Name, Phone Number, and Email

Permission to Contact (Yes/No)

You can list your internships in the same section as your work experiences, or you can separate them so that they are clearly defined. Your internship experiences demonstrate qualification for a position whether they were paid or unpaid. You can acquire credit that may qualify you at a higher grade level. Be sure to add hours per week so you can get credit for this experience.

Work and School Projects and Accomplishments

If your jobs or internships were project-based, you should describe each project. Expressing achievement in the workplace is an excellent way to stand out from the competition.

Project Lists

Keep notes on your projects, and record your accomplishments for your resume, KSAs, and interviews.

Track the following:

- ⟶ Title of project/program
- ⟶ Mission or objective
- ⟶ Your role
- ⟶ People with whom you communicated
- ⟶ Major challenges or problems
- ⟶ Results (products including reports, cost savings, improved efficiency, a particular service, etc.)

Accomplishments in Job Descriptions and Major Accomplishment Sections

Even if your job does not involve special projects, you should highlight accomplishments. Do this by literally listing selected accomplishments at the end of a job description set off by a sub-heading. If you have achieved something special, large, or important in your career or life that you want to emphasize, you can create a "Major Accomplishments" section after the relevant jobs.

Include Recognitions

- ⟶ Team reviews
- ⟶ Professor reviews
- ⟶ Articles from newspapers
- ⟶ Awards
- ⟶ Letters of recognition

Don't just use your private industry resume to apply for federal jobs. The federal resume must be longer (3 to 5 pages) to provide enough information for the Federal HR specialist to determine whether you meet the job qualifications.

Other Information

Other information includes community service, special interests or hobbies, or information about skills and accomplishments that doesn't fit elsewhere. Contrary to popular belief, such listings are not "fluff" and, if done properly, can even be an asset. HR personnel reading your resume may remember you specifically because of your outside interests. In practical terms, other information probably has the least direct relevance to the job you're applying for, so this section should be placed last on a federal resume. However, such placement does have the advantage of being the last thing a reader may see, and perhaps has the potential to create an impact.

See samples of student resumes starting on page 101, and get started with yours!

The Best Federal Resume Format

The Outline Format Federal Resume is the easiest format to read for busy human resources specialists. USAJOBS is a "human-read" system where an actual human resources person will read your resume for the specialized experience, KSAs, and keywords from the job announcement. Key points of the Outline Format Federal Resume:

⇢ Use small paragraphs for readability; writing style is narrative and descriptive
⇢ Match your resume with ALL CAPS keywords from the announcement
⇢ Add accomplishments with specific details to prove your experience
⇢ May be copied and pasted into the USAJOBS resume builder or uploaded
⇢ Proves the Knowledge, Skills, and Abilities as listed in the USAJOBS announcement

Excerpts shown here are from Philip Sang's resumes on pages 109 and 112

Sample of the Outline Format Keywords in ALL CAPS

ENGINEERING TECHNICIAN (Intern), GS-0802-05   05/2011-08/2011
United States Coast Guard, Civil Engineering Unit, Honolulu, HI 96850   Hours/week: 40
Supervisor: Neal Kamona, Phone: 808-444-4444, May contact

- APPLIED ENGINEERING PRINCIPLES AND CONCEPT KNOWLEDGE to evaluate designs for $5M C-130 Hercules rinse rack that complied with military regulations and FAA height restrictions. Researched concepts that incorporated a reverse-osmosis water-filtration system to reclaim used water to reduce water usage and that required minimal maintenance over system lifetime.

- COMMUNICATED ORALLY AND IN WRITING. Worked closely with engineers, senior and support staff and stakeholders. Coordinated meetings with contracting companies regarding site preparation for C-130 rinse rack at the local air station. Contacted State of Hawai'i officials to obtain as-built drawings for a floating dock project that was slated to moor a pair of 100-foot Coast Guard cutters; coordinated site visits to assess ocean swell conditions at the State of Hawai'i floating dock and assessed the dock's performance.

- USED TECHNICAL SKILLS to update and maintain engineering drawing database by filing as-built, engineering and surveying drawings with proper descriptions of each drawing.

Sample of the Bullet Format for Private Industry

ENGINEERING TECHNICIAN (Intern), GS-0802-05   05/2011-08/2011
United States Coast Guard, Civil Engineering Unit, Honolulu, HI;   Hours/week: 40

- Evaluated designs for $5M C-130 Hercules rinse rack that complied with military regulations and FAA height restrictions.
- Researched concepts that incorporated a reverse-osmosis water-filtration system to reclaim used water to reduce water usage and that required minimal maintenance over system lifetime.
- Worked closely with engineers, senior and support staff and stakeholders.
- Coordinated meetings with contracting companies regarding site preparation for C-130 rinse rack at the local air station. Contacted State of Hawai'i officials to obtain as-built drawings for a floating dock project that was slated to moor a pair of 100-foot Coast Guard cutters.
- Coordinated site visits to assess ocean swell conditions at the State of Hawai'i floating dock and assessed the dock's performance.
- Updated and maintained engineering drawing database by filing as-built, engineering and surveying drawings with proper descriptions of each drawing.

STEP 7: KSAs, Questionnaires, and Cover Letters

Additional Student Veterans info on page 91

Give Yourself All the Credit You Can in Part 2 of Your Application

⟶ KSA narratives were eliminated by the Hiring Reform of May 2010, but KSAs are still part of the federal application, just not as separate narratives (usually)

⟶ Write your KSA accomplishments inside your resume

⟶ Match your resume to your answers in the Questionnaire

⟶ Prepare accomplishments for your interview

⟶ Write a compelling cover letter

SAMPLE PATHWAYS ANNOUNCEMENT

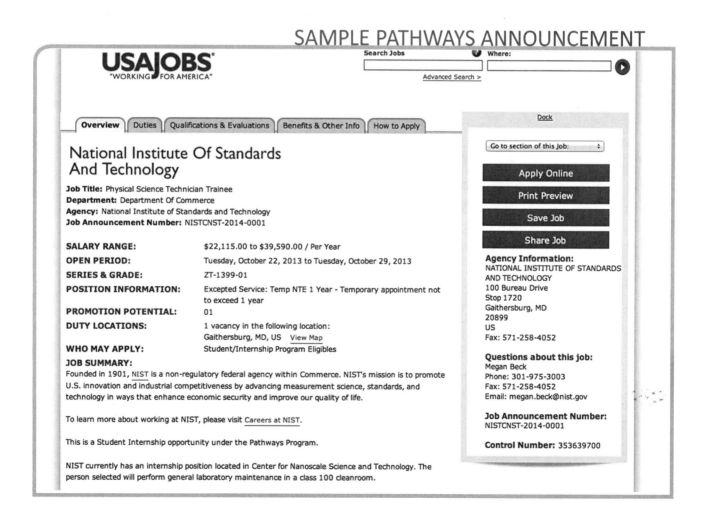

What is a KSA?

KSA is an acronym for "Knowledge, Skills, and Abilities." Up until May 2010, most federal applications required KSA narratives in addition to submitting the federal resume. President Obama's Hiring Reform eliminated the requirement for the written narratives as the first part of a federal application.

However, KSA narratives can still be seen in 4 places in a federal job application.

1. **Qualification Section of the USAJOBS Announcement.** Knowledge, Skills, and Abilities are listed in many of the Qualifications sections of the USAJOBS vacancy announcements. Jobseekers should now cover their knowledge, skills, and abilities in the federal resume, rather than in separate narratives

2. **Questionnaires.** The KSAs are also covered in the Questionnaires. You will need to select your skill level in a multiple-choice or Yes/No format. The questionnaires are scored automatically and will become part of your application

3. **Technical Qualifications or KSAs requiring separate written narratives.** Sometimes there are KSAs or Technical Qualifications where you still have to write separate narratives

4. **Behavior-Based Interviews.** The KSAs are also usually included in the federal job interview. So reading and covering the KSAs in the resume and the questionnaire will be good practice for the job interview

KSAs in the Qualifications Section of the Announcements

KSAs are listed in the vacancy announcements, but often are called different things like "Accomplishments," "Technical Qualifications," Quality Ranking Factors," or "Statements of Qualifications." Whatever the title of the KSAs, applicants must address them in their resume.

Sample KSA Requirements in Qualification Section:

The position requires knowledge of, and skill in applying, a comprehensive body of HR rules, procedures, and technical methods sufficient to: 1) Carry out limited technical projects; 2) Analyze a variety of routine facts; 3) Research minor complaints or problems that are not readily understood; and 4) Summarize HR facts and issues.

KSA Topics

The new KSA accomplishments are designed to solicit detailed information about your training and experience to aid HR professionals in making qualitative distinctions among eligible applicants. They are used to "weed out" the less qualified applicants, and to move the better qualified ones closer to the interview stage. Covering the KSA statements in the resume also prepares you for potential interviews. When combined with the "duties and responsibilities" portion of a vacancy announcement, an awareness of KSAs improves your ability to field any questions that a federal hiring manager may ask.

One Size Does Not Fit All

Be prepared to meet a wide variety of KSA topics. KSAs can be concrete knowlege, or soft skills. They can be highly specific to the position at hand, or a general ability that most positions require.

The Most Common KSAs

"Communication" is an important skill for most jobs; therefore, KSAs involving communication are common. Here are some examples of communication KSAs, ranging from simple to complex:

- Skill in oral communications
- Skill in written communications
- Skill in written and oral communications
- Demonstrated ability to communicate technical results in a variety of formats (including oral presentations and publications) for both technical and non-technical audiences

Job-specific knowledge is another common KSA topic. Here are some samples:
- Basic knowledge of concepts, principles, and practices in the electrical engineering field
- Professional knowledge of and skill in applying accounting concepts, principles, and methods
- Knowledge of laws, regulations and procedures governing employment (staffing, pay, and employee benefits)
- Knowledge of health care systems and the role of Medicare, Medicaid, and other CMS programs in providing health care services to the nation's beneficiaries
- Knowledge of major statistical computer packages and languages, including SAS, to be used to produce final results from data using appropriate statistical theory

GOOD NEWS FOR INTERNSHIP APPLICATIONS:
Federal internship announcements usually do not require KSAs, but could become part of the internship interview.

Strategies for Writing KSAs

Tip #1: Reframe the KSA into an interview question

To help you get started writing, use your imagination to re-think the KSA as a question, as if you were being interviewed.

KSA Example:	Basic knowledge of concepts, principles, and practices in the electrical engineering field.
Reframe as a question:	Can you give me an example of how you utilized your basic knowledge of the concepts, principles, and practices in the field of electrical engineering?
KSA Example:	Skill in written and oral communications.
Reframe as a question:	Can you describe an example of how you demonstrated your skills in written and oral communications?

Tip #2: Pull examples from your college courses, work, internships or life experiences

You know that saying, "Life is what happens while you're making other plans"? You don't have to always draw from work experience! Students gain their knowledge, skills and abilities from many sources. As long as it's an example that demonstrates the knowledge, skill, or ability being assessed, it's fair game.

Here are some examples:

- Class papers
- Exams with essays or take-home exams
- Work Study
- Summer jobs
- Clubs
- Hobbies
- Family life
- Presentations
- Special projects
- Internships
- Volunteer positions
- Student government
- Religious experience

Tip #3: Remember that your federal resume will be scored into a category of Best Qualified, Well Qualified, or Qualified

Your KSA accomplishments can help your resume to score in the Best Qualified Category. For the behavior-based interview, each accomplishment is "rated" against a crediting plan that the Managers develop. The rating, or score, is based on:

- How well you demonstrate your knowledge, skill, or ability in that area
- Your level of skill "usage"
- The examples used in your CCAR stories

KSA Rating Scale

Have you wondered how KSAs are rated? The following example of a rating method for INTERPERSONAL SKILLS will give you some insight to help you write your KSAs.

Benchmark Level	Level Definition	Level Examples
5	Establishes and maintains ongoing working relationships with management, other employees, internal or external stakeholders, or customers. Remains courteous when discussing information or eliciting highly sensitive or controversial information from people who are reluctant to give it. Effectively handles situations involving a high degree of tension or discomfort involving people who are demonstrating a high degree of hostility or distress.	Presents controversial findings tactfully to irate organization senior management officials regarding shortcomings of a newly installed computer system, software programs, and associated equipment.
4		Mediates disputes concerning system design/architecture, the nature and capacity of data management systems, system resources allocations, or other equally controversial sensitive matters.
3	Cooperates and works well with management, other employees or customers, or short-term assignments. Remains courteous when discussing information or eliciting moderately sensitive or controversial information from people who are hesitant to give it. Effectively handles situations involving a moderate degree of tension or discomfort involving people who are demonstrating a moderate degree of hostility or distress.	Courteously and tactfully delivers effective instruction to frustrated customers. Provides technical advice to customers and the public on various types of IT such as communication or security systems, data management procedures or analysis, software engineering, or web development.
2		Familiarizes new employees with administrative procedures and office systems.
1	Cooperates and works well with management, other employees, or customers during brief interactions. Remains courteous when discussing information or eliciting non-sensitive or non-controversial information from people who are willing to give it. Effectively handles situations involving little or no tension, discomfort, hostility, or distress	Responds courteously to customers' general inquiries. Greets and assists visitors attending a meeting within own organization.

Sample KSA

KSA: Ability to communicate orally.

Context: I orally presented the culmination of my group's work on the Rwandan genocide to our graduate class in Non-profit Management.

Challenge: The presentation was particularly challenging because, after our team spent months analyzing a very complex problem, I was given 15 minutes to present the problem, our group's analyses, and our recommendations. While we worked collaboratively to sort out the issues and recommendations, in the end, I was left to develop an organized presentation outline and script within the time limits.

Action 1: To begin the project, my group conducted intensive research on the timeline of events in Rwanda.

Action 2: My research component focused on the management structures of the United Nations. I utilized official documents from multiple international governments and intergovernmental organizations. For the presentation, we developed a summary of events, analysis of the crisis, and specific management recommendations.

Action 3: Using PowerPoint, I presented the history of the Rwanda genocide, my analysis of management failures, and recommendations for change within the United Nations.

Action 4: I also answered questions from the audience.

Results: My 15-minute presentation was positively received by the class. Many people were moved by the story of Rwanda. They were also shocked when we revealed how simple flaws in management structure led to a travesty of justice. Our presentation received an excellent grade, and our professor complimented me for the clarity and succinct nature of my presentation.

Most USAJOBS postings include "Part 2" of the application, the questionnaire. Give yourself as much credit as possible, and make sure your resume matches your answers.

Cover Letters

Communicate Your Enthusiasm

You want the hiring agent to know that you are highly motivated and hope to attain the position. You can communicate this with an upbeat tone or style. To do this, write a draft and read it out loud enthusiastically. Does it sound right or does the language you use sound strange when you try to act upbeat while reading it?

No matter how good an actor you might be, the line, "In my opinion, I have qualifications that make me an appropriate candidate for this position," does not sound natural. Try it. The following line is better and could fit in an upbeat letter: "One reason I am eager to work in this position is that my qualifications exactly match the requirements of the job."

While keeping "upbeat" in mind, you must also remember to maintain a professional image. The line, "I am so well qualified for this position it's amazing!" is over the top. Ask someone else to read your draft of the cover letter and tell you if you have balanced enthusiasm with a professional statement of why you should be hired for the job. Most importantly, be true to your personality!

Summarize Why You Are the Ideal Candidate for the Job

You can state why you are ideal for the job by literally listing the reasons. Just in case you are unable to think of them, check out this list and see which ones might apply to you:
- → Your knowledge, skills, and abilities
- → Your experience and training
- → Your core competencies, like being able to work independently, in teams, under pressure, or creatively
- → Your desire to support the agency mission
- → Your desire to work for the particular office
- → Your desire to help the particular customer base
- → Your desire to live in that location
- → The duties and responsibilities appeal to you
- → The position fits into your long-term career goals
- → Your desire to serve your country

See sample cover letters starting on page 153

Explain Any Unusual Circumstances

The last purpose of the cover letter is to explain any unusual circumstances if necessary. These might include gaps in your career timeline, disabilities and accommodations required, conflicts of interest, or anything you think they should know. If you think something on your resume might be considered unusual but you are not certain, you should ask friends in your network if they would include it in the letter.

STUDENTS FEDERAL CAREER GUIDE

STEP 8: Submit Your Application

Additional Student Veterans
info on page 91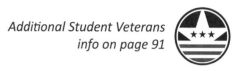

When applying for federal jobs, there are five important things to know:

⇢ Follow the directions of the vacancy announcement
⇢ Know the deadline
⇢ Effectively format your information for online applications
⇢ Be prepared to submit several documents by email or fax
⇢ Be prepared to wait and to ask questions

SAMPLE PATHWAYS ANNOUNCEMENT

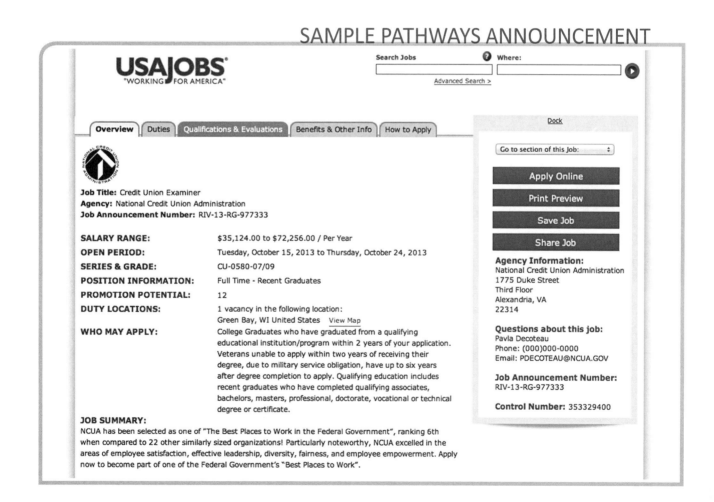

Federal Job Applications Are Challenging

The federal job market is significantly different from the private sector. As previously discussed, job terminology varies between the two; federal resumes are more detailed and complex to prepare, and a response to your federal application can take months. At first glance this can be intimidating. Novice federal jobseekers may try to use materials they have prepared for the private sector, but they won't get far.

One reason the federal job search process is so exhaustive is that your application package represents an examination (with actual grading) of your qualifications. Also, the federal application process is more focused on the front end of the process—the resumes and document section—as opposed to the private sector, which spends more time in the interviewing stage. This is mostly due to the many rules the government needs to follow to ensure fairness in the hiring process. It is also due to the sheer number of applicants. Hiring officials are always looking for ways to reduce the number of applicants.

This step gives you information on how to avoid being rejected before your application is even considered. These suggestions apply to internships, too.

Give yourself plenty of time to complete an application. It can take more time than you think to target your resume toward the announcement, complete the questionnaire, and submit the necessary documents.

Important Application Tips

Follow the Directions in the Vacancy Announcement

Never deviate from the written instructions on a federal vacancy announcement for any reason.

Know the Deadline

Applications for federal job vacancies will be accepted only while the vacancy is "open." Open periods can be as short as a few days, or they can go on indefinitely. These are set by the agencies, and represent your window for applying for the job. The closing date is the last day applications will be accepted. It will be clearly indicated on the announcement.

If you happen to find a vacancy announcement at the last minute, one that you just have to apply for, the exact time of day on the closing date can be important. Many vacancy announcements, especially those on web-based systems, close at midnight on the deadline. Be mindful of how the date and time are expressed.

Some announcements that require emailed or faxed applications close at 5 p.m. on the deadline. Others need to be postmarked on that day. If you are mailing your application, you will want to know if your package must be received or postmarked by the closing date. The difference between these two is huge. Often, supplemental materials, like transcripts, can be submitted shortly after the closing date.

Online Applications

For electronic applications, complete all of the pages and questions. Sometimes there are at least 3 steps to applying: Profile/Registration; Resume Builder or Resume Submission; and Questions or Essays. Be sure you do not exceed the maximum number of characters allowed in a field. There's very little formatting that you can do within text fields, but make entries as easy to read as possible. Make sure you finish the submission. Do not close the application screen until you have clicked a "Finish" or "Submit" button. You should receive an email or see on your account page that the application was submitted successfully.

Timing: How Long Does It Take to Get Hired?

Currently, the waiting time is likely to be about 80 days. The following chart illustrates the path of your resume from the initial review system to the supervisor who can decide to interview you for the position.

How Federal Job Applications Are Processed

Key steps in federal hiring that involve job applicants' interaction

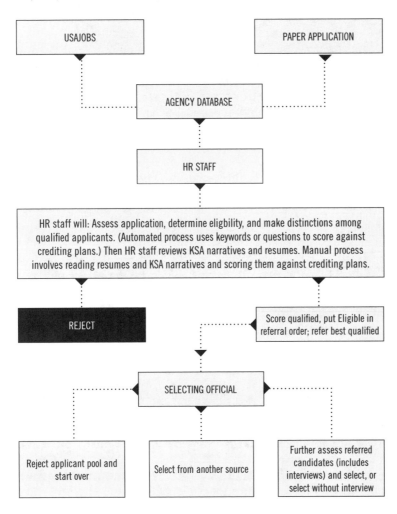

STEP 9: Track and Follow Up

Additional Student Veterans
info on page 91
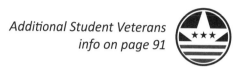

You Can Track Your Applications with USAJOBS.gov and Applicationmanager.gov

⇢ Should I wait to hear from the agency?
⇢ Can I track the progress of my application?
⇢ How do I advocate for my applications with HR professionals effectively?

SAMPLE PATHWAYS ANNOUNCEMENT

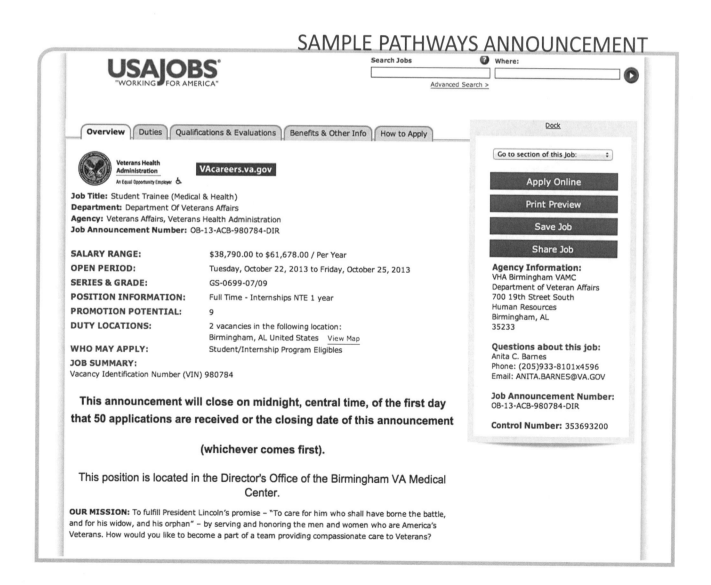

USAJOBS "WORKING FOR AMERICA"

Search Jobs   Where: Advanced Search >

| Overview | Duties | Qualifications & Evaluations | Benefits & Other Info | How to Apply |

Veterans Health Administration An Equal Opportunity Employer

VAcareers.va.gov

Job Title: Student Trainee (Medical & Health)
Department: Department Of Veterans Affairs
Agency: Veterans Affairs, Veterans Health Administration
Job Announcement Number: OB-13-ACB-980784-DIR

SALARY RANGE:	$38,790.00 to $61,678.00 / Per Year
OPEN PERIOD:	Tuesday, October 22, 2013 to Friday, October 25, 2013
SERIES & GRADE:	GS-0699-07/09
POSITION INFORMATION:	Full Time - Internships NTE 1 year
PROMOTION POTENTIAL:	9
DUTY LOCATIONS:	2 vacancies in the following location: Birmingham, AL United States View Map
WHO MAY APPLY:	Student/Internship Program Eligibles

JOB SUMMARY:
Vacancy Identification Number (VIN) 980784

This announcement will close on midnight, central time, of the first day that 50 applications are received or the closing date of this announcement

(whichever comes first).

This position is located in the Director's Office of the Birmingham VA Medical Center.

OUR MISSION: To fulfill President Lincoln's promise – "To care for him who shall have borne the battle, and for his widow, and his orphan" – by serving and honoring the men and women who are America's Veterans. How would you like to become a part of a team providing compassionate care to Veterans?

Dock

Go to section of this Job:

Apply Online
Print Preview
Save Job
Share Job

Agency Information:
VHA Birmingham VAMC
Department of Veteran Affairs
700 19th Street South
Human Resources
Birmingham, AL
35233

Questions about this job:
Anita C. Barnes
Phone: (205)933-8101x4596
Email: ANITA.BARNES@VA.GOV

Job Announcement Number:
OB-13-ACB-980784-DIR

Control Number: 353693200

Can I Contact Them?

Yes, you can, and you should!

Waiting to hear news of an application can be the hardest part of any internship or job search. It can be especially frustrating with federal positions because it can take months.

This step gives you some suggestions on how to help your application maneuver through the system and give you some peace of mind.

Most federal job applicants are not aware that they can contact the HR personnel handling their application. Asking questions, gaining information, developing a relationship, and becoming known are a helpful part of the application process. You can track most of the steps your application follows through the system. Some of the online application systems are even set up to ensure that you will be contacted.

Vacancy announcements typically include the name of a human resources professional who is responsible for many aspects of the application process. This HR person may have created the vacancy announcement, posted it on USAJOBS and other websites, and may communicate with the hiring supervisor. They may coordinate the review of the packages and be part of the rating and ranking process to determine who will get an interview. This HR person is a great resource for you. Refer back to the Federal Hiring Chart in Step 8 on page 78 to review how central this HR person is in the process.

Just a reminder, they are busy!
Human resources staff are occupied with multiple announcements, various aspects of announcement development, reviewing packages, and responding to supervisor needs. Use diplomacy and consideration when contacting them about your application. Your goal is to be remembered favorably!

Suggested Follow-Up Scripts

First Message – 30 days after the closing date

"Hi, Ms. Rogers, this is Emily Troutman from San Diego, CA. I'm inquiring about my application for Writer-Editor, GS-7, announcement 20205, which I submitted on April 5, 20xx. I'd like to know the status of my application, or when the applications are being reviewed. Can you please return my call or leave a voicemail at (410) 777-7777. The best time to reach me is 11 a.m. to 1 p.m. Eastern Time. My email is etrout171@gmail.com. Thank you very much."

AFTER the Interview – THANK YOU NOTE!

Dear Ms. Rogers:
Thank you so much for your time last Wednesday. I enjoyed meeting you and hearing about your agency. I believe that I would be an asset to your organization and feel certain that I would be able to learn quickly about your mission and programs. I look forward to your decision and hope that I can begin my career at the Office of _____ at Department of _____.

Sincerely, Emily Troutman

Following up will help you get the information you need to improve your future applications.

Sample Questions for Applicants to Ask HR

1. Can you clarify something from the announcement for me?

If you don't understand a certain request of the vacancy announcement, ask for clarification. If the person you're talking to isn't the named contact person, be sure to get his or her name.

2. Have you received all my materials?

Many vacancy announcements require you to submit materials by different methods. For example, you may have to use a USAStaffing online application system which follows two steps: 1) submit information online, and 2) fax or mail your transcripts. It's a good idea to check to see if all your materials have been received before the closing date. Some electronic application systems list the status of your application materials. If you mail any materials, remember to save your receipts.

3. What is the status of my application?

The federal job application process can take a while. You can call to check on the status of your application, but we suggest that you wait about a month after the closing date. You may learn that you did or did not get on the list submitted to the selecting official, or that interviews are being conducted.

While you wait, you can keep track of your application on USAJOBS, at *www.applicationmanager.gov*, AvueCentral, or any other web system the agency uses. It is a good idea to know what these sites say about your application before you contact HR.

4. How can I improve future applications?

This is REALLY IMPORTANT. If you learn that you didn't get referred for a position, ask the contact person to tell you what you should do to improve future applications. You may learn that you missed a selective factor. You may learn that you weren't qualified for a particular grade. You may learn that you didn't score highly on your questionnaire. You may also learn that you scored very well, but were in competition with a highly qualified group of applicants.

The HR representative usually will not go into great detail, but may tell you what your overall score was, where your application was weak, and where you ranked among the pool of applicants. If you didn't get the job you were seeking, then talking on the phone with the people who read and scored your materials can be the most valuable five or ten minutes you can spend in this whole process.

STEP 10: Interview for a Federal Job

Additional Student Veterans info on page 91
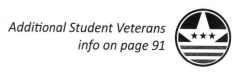

The federal job interview is an examination. Be prepared.

⇢ Learn the agency's mission
⇢ Be prepared to give examples of your courses and projects
⇢ Practice your examples before the interview

SAMPLE PATHWAYS ANNOUNCEMENT

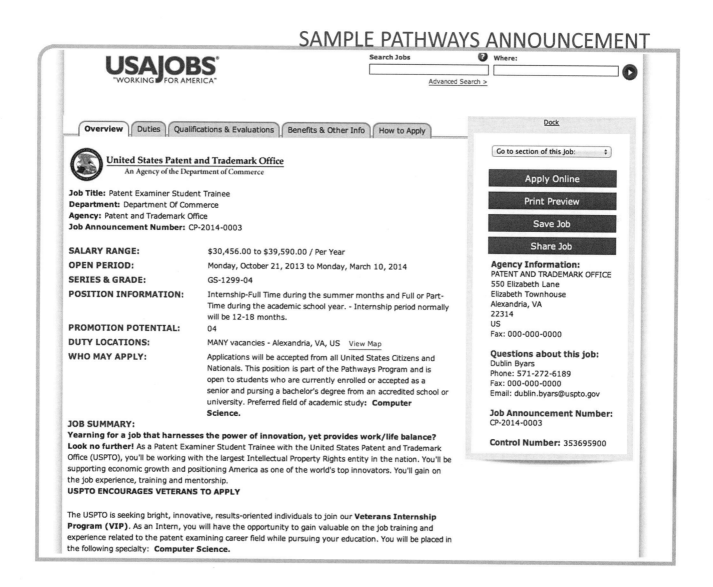

USAJOBS
"WORKING FOR AMERICA"

Search Jobs
Where:
Advanced Search >

| Overview | Duties | Qualifications & Evaluations | Benefits & Other Info | How to Apply |

United States Patent and Trademark Office
An Agency of the Department of Commerce

Job Title: Patent Examiner Student Trainee
Department: Department Of Commerce
Agency: Patent and Trademark Office
Job Announcement Number: CP-2014-0003

SALARY RANGE:	$30,456.00 to $39,590.00 / Per Year
OPEN PERIOD:	Monday, October 21, 2013 to Monday, March 10, 2014
SERIES & GRADE:	GS-1299-04
POSITION INFORMATION:	Internship-Full Time during the summer months and Full or Part-Time during the academic school year. - Internship period normally will be 12-18 months.
PROMOTION POTENTIAL:	04
DUTY LOCATIONS:	MANY vacancies - Alexandria, VA, US View Map
WHO MAY APPLY:	Applications will be accepted from all United States Citizens and Nationals. This position is part of the Pathways Program and is open to students who are currently enrolled or accepted as a senior and pursing a bachelor's degree from an accredited school or university. Preferred field of academic study: **Computer Science**.

JOB SUMMARY:
Yearning for a job that harnesses the power of innovation, yet provides work/life balance?
Look no further! As a Patent Examiner Student Trainee with the United States Patent and Trademark Office (USPTO), you'll be working with the largest Intellectual Property Rights entity in the nation. You'll be supporting economic growth and positioning America as one of the world's top innovators. You'll gain on the job experience, training and mentorship.
USPTO ENCOURAGES VETERANS TO APPLY

The USPTO is seeking bright, innovative, results-oriented individuals to join our **Veterans Internship Program (VIP)**. As an Intern, you will have the opportunity to gain valuable on the job training and experience related to the patent examining career field while pursuing your education. You will be placed in the following specialty: **Computer Science.**

Dock

Go to section of this Job:

Apply Online
Print Preview
Save Job
Share Job

Agency Information:
PATENT AND TRADEMARK OFFICE
550 Elizabeth Lane
Elizabeth Townhouse
Alexandria, VA
22314
US
Fax: 000-000-0000

Questions about this job:
Dublin Byars
Phone: 571-272-6189
Fax: 000-000-0000
Email: dublin.byars@uspto.gov

Job Announcement Number:
CP-2014-0003

Control Number: 353695900

Congratulations! You've Been Selected for an Interview!

The federal government uses many different approaches to interviewing. This section will help you understand these approaches and provide some practical tips on preparing for interviews.

Managers vary their interviewing techniques and processes to develop an understanding of you as a candidate for their position. The interview will depend on the type of position, as well as the information the manager needs to determine if you are the best "fit".

Interviews for students or interns may be, in many ways, no different from regular employment interviews. You may be asked about your long-term career goals, your interest in the position and the agency, and your long and short-term education plans. Be ready to discuss your current or previous courses and what you are learning.

Interviews for students and interns may be, in many ways, no different from regular employment interviews.

Interviews may be conducted in person or over the phone, and may include an interview panel. There are three main interview methods:

⇢ Behavioral
⇢ Case/Hypothetical
⇢ Technical

You need to know the type of interview in which you will be participating. When you are contacted for the interview, it is appropriate for you to request information regarding the type and method of interviewing that will be conducted and with whom you will be meeting.

Types of Interviews

Behavior Interviews

Employers use behavioral style interviews to predict your future performance from your past behavior in settings and situations related to the position at hand. Applicants are asked questions that require them to tell stories and give examples of their abilities, much like KSAs. Here are some examples:

→ Describe a time when you were under pressure to make a decision. How did you react?

→ Can you think of a problem or situation that you have encountered, where the old solutions simply didn't work, and when you came up with a new solution(s)?

→ Are you a risk-taker or do you prefer to play it safe? Give an example of when you had to take a risk and one when you had to play it safe.

→ What changes have you made in your life and why? Which are you most proud of?

Tips for preparing for a behavioral interview:

→ Prior to the interview, spend some time identifying behaviors that would be critical to success in the position—and do an honest assessment!

→ Do a Google search and look for behavioral interview questions—and practice!

→ Spend some time thinking through mistakes you have made in the workplace. What would you do differently—in other words, how would you change your behavior the next time?

Practice makes perfect.
Find someone to practice on!

Case/Hypothetical Interviews

Case and hypothetical interviews are situational in nature and are designed to see how interviewees will respond to different situations, how well they think on their feet, and whether they are good at problem solving. Examples of these are:

⇢ Your supervisor has left an assignment for you, but has left on vacation for a week. The assignment is due when she returns. You don't completely understand the assignment—what would you do?

⇢ You have been responsible for dealing with a particularly challenging client, who has indicated in their latest phone call that they are thinking of taking their business someplace else. How would you handle the situation?

⇢ The successful candidate for this position will be working with some highly-trained individuals who have been with the organization for a long time. How will you approach them?

Tips for preparing for a case or hypothetical interview:

⇢ Spend some time thinking about mistakes you have made on the job or in school. How would you explain them to an interviewer, and what have you learned from those mistakes?

⇢ Research the organization's website to identify organizational competencies and values, and assess how you would fit into the organization.

⇢ Research practice questions and work with peers or counselors to practice responding to questions.

Technical Interviews

Technical interviews are focused on providing the selecting official with additional information regarding the technical or functional skills of the applicant.

⇢ Describe your experience with accounting principles, practices, and techniques

⇢ Describe your experience in applying program management theories and processes

⇢ This position requires experience in scientific research—provide us with information on your role and/or participation in performing basic and/or applied research

⇢ How do you keep abreast of new developments in your profession or industry? On a scale of 1-10, how up-to-date are you?

⇢ How does your degree in (major) prepare you for a career in (occupation/industry), or to excel as a (position title)?

⇢ In your current job/school situation, what types of decisions do you make without consulting your immediate supervisor?

⇢ On a scale of 1-5, how would you assess your technical skills and why?

Tips for preparing for a technical interview:

⇢ Closely review the technical requirements listed in the vacancy announcement and develop a mental inventory of your skills for each requirement

⇢ Identify questions you may have regarding the technical requirements of the work— this will demonstrate your technical skill level

⇢ Check with college professors, peers, and counselors regarding information on the technical challenges and issues facing the organization; develop scenarios for problem-solving

Interview Tips

Before the Interview

--→ Be prepared!

--→ Check out the website of the agency you're interviewing with and conduct research (size, services, products, etc.)

--→ Prepare a one-minute response to the "Tell me about yourself" question

--→ Be memorable! Media training expert TJ Walker from _www.worldwidemedia. com_ recommends that you have a story or message prepared so that you will be remembered at the "water cooler"

--→ Try to find out what kind of interview to expect (i.e., behavioral, technical, etc.). Feel free to ask when scheduling the interview

--→ Write five success stories to answer behavioral interview questions ("Tell me about a time when..." or "Give me an example of a time...")

--→ Prepare answers to the most common interview questions that will best present your skills, talents, and accomplishments:

- Why did you leave your last position?

- What do you know about our organization?

- What are your goals/Where do you see yourself in 5 years?

- What are your strengths? What are your weaknesses/areas of improvement?

- Why would you like to work for this organization?

- What is your most significant achievement?

- How would your last boss/colleagues/friends describe you?

- Why should we hire you?

- What are your salary expectations?

--→ Remember, nothing will make you look worse than not knowing what you put on your own resume

--→ Have 5-10 high-quality questions prepared for the interviewer. Only ask the ones that were not addressed during your discussion

--→ Practice in front of a mirror or with a friend for feedback

--→ Have your references' permission. These might be former managers, professors, or people who know you through community service. You want them to be prepared to praise you. It would be beneficial to provide your references with the following information: the job for which you are applying, the name of the organization, and a copy of your resume

During the Interview

→ Arrive 10 to 15 minutes early for your interview

→ Dress appropriately! Ironed clothes, including skirts (at knee length or longer), nice slacks, or a suit. Keep your interview outfit simple and professional. Be conservative (until you get hired)

→ Carry these items to the interview:
  • a copy of your references (for which you already have permission)
  • paper on which to take notes
  • directions to the interview site
  • a copy of your resume
  • a pen

→ Be aware of your body language and eye contact. Stand and greet your interviewer with a firm handshake and a smile. Crossed arms appear to be defensive, fidgeting may make everyone nervous, and lack of eye contact may be interpreted as untrustworthiness. Instead, nod while listening to show you are attentive and alert, and most importantly, sit and stand up straight

Think before you answer; if you do not have a clear understanding of a question, ask for clarification

Show a sincere interest in the office and position. (You already know about the organization, as you already conducted your research)

→ Express yourself clearly and with confidence, not conceit. Keep your answers concise and to the point

→ Focus on what you can contribute to the organization rather than what the employer can do for you. Don't ask about salary or benefits until the employer brings it up

→ Try not to talk about politics (don't bring it up yourself). Talk about your skills and experience, but don't start a political discussion

→ Do not place blame on or be negative about past employers

→ End the interview on an positive note indicating how you feel you are a good fit for the position at hand, and how you can make a contribution to the organization. Ask about the next step, as most offers are not extended on the spot

→ Thank the interviewer and ask for a business card (this will provide you with the necessary contact information)

After the Interview

Thank you letters should be written graciously, promptly, and carefully. Think about the best form for your thank you. If the interviewer tells you he/she plans to make a decision that night, then you should email promptly. At the same time, if you are applying to an agency that prides itself on doing personalized work for clients, you may want to send a handwritten message on a nice card. Either way, thank the interviewer for his/her time, gently reminding them of your interest in the position, and the valuable contributions you would bring to the organization. Do not miss that last chance to market yourself!

Student Veterans

SAMPLE PATHWAYS ANNOUNCEMENT

USAJOBS®
"WORKING FOR AMERICA"

Search Jobs   Where:

Advanced Search >

< Back to Results

Dock

| Overview | Duties | Qualifications & Evaluations | Benefits & Other Info | How to Apply |

Go to section of this Job:

Apply Online

Print Preview

Save Job

Share Job

CIVILIAN CAREERS

REAL-WORLD CHALLENGES   **REAL-LIFE** REWARDS
DEPARTMENT OF THE NAVY

Job Title: DON Recent Graduate Program (Supply Systems Analyst)
Department: Department of the Navy
Agency: Naval Supply Systems Command
Job Announcement Number: NE32003-11-981014L4693756-P

SALARY RANGE:	$38,790.00 to $50,431.00 / Per Year
OPEN PERIOD:	Friday, October 25, 2013 to Monday, October 28, 2013
SERIES & GRADE:	GS-2003-07
POSITION INFORMATION:	Full Time - Recent Graduates
PROMOTION POTENTIAL:	11
DUTY LOCATIONS:	1 vacancy in the following location: Naval Support Activity, Mechanicsburg, PA View Map
WHO MAY APPLY:	Recent Graduates in the following counties in Pennsylvania: Cumberland, Perry, Dauphin, York, Adams, Lancaster, Franklin, Lebanon, Juniata, Huntingdon, Snyder,Centre and Northumberland.

Agency Information:
Navy OCHR Philadelphia Ops Center
700 Robbins Avenue
Philadelphia, PA
19111

Questions about this job:
DON Employment Info Center EIC
Phone: (800)378-4559
Email: DONEIC@NAVY.MIL

Job Announcement Number:
NE32003-11-981014L4693756-P

Control Number: 353733900

JOB SUMMARY:
The Navy and Marine Corps team offers innovative, exciting and meaningful work linking military and civilian talents to achieve our mission and safeguard our freedoms. Department of the Navy provides competitive salaries, comprehensive benefits, and extensive professional development and training. From pipefitters to accountants, scientists to engineers, doctors to nurses-the careers and opportunities to make a difference are endless. Civilian careers-where purpose and patriotism unite!

Additional Benefits for Student Veterans Applying for Internships and Federal Jobs

Thank You for Your Service to America! Veterans Have Great Tuition, Book, and Housing Benefits for Going to College

For your service to America, you have earned valuable education benefits. These programs are for active duty military, separated or retired veterans, and spouses and children of military. Use the benefits while on active duty ... or after active duty.

In order to be 100% eligible for the Post-9/11 GI Bill, you must have served at least 36 months that were not obligated service time to any other benefit (such as attending one of the academies or the loan repayment program). You can take advantage of Post-9/11 GI Bill benefits prior to the 36-month mark at lower rates. For example, after 90 days of service, you would be eligible at 40%. The percentage of maximum benefit payable increases with the length of active duty, up to 36 months at 100%.

Need education, training, or certification to begin your new career?
Your tuition, housing, and books can be fully covered...up to $52,000 for 36 months. Typically, the GI Bill will pay for the most expensive public institution in any state. For private colleges, the VA has a national cap—for 2013, the cap was set at $18,077.50—which is indexed to the rising cost of tuition nationally.

Yellow Ribbon Program. Need extra funding?
The Yellow Ribbon Program can provide additional funding for college tuition if the tuition is higher than the Post-9/11 GI Bill tuition cap. The Yellow Ribbon Program is a yearly contract between the Department of Veterans Affairs and an individual school that elects to participate. For more information about the Yellow Ribbon Program, call the Department of Veterans Affairs, visit the Department of Veterans Affairs website, or contact the school directly. A list of Yellow Ribbon participating institutions is available at *http://gibill.va.gov/ benefits/post_911_gibill/yellow_ribbon_program.html*.

Timing is everything. Remember to assign your benefits while you are still on active duty.
If you want to transfer your benefits to a dependent, you must assign the benefits while you are still on active duty. Your GI Bill tuition benefits, or portions of the 36 months, can be assigned to your spouse or children.

MORE TUITION BENEFITS INFORMATION
Contact your military base education office.
Your selected college veteran's representative can be found at: *http://gibill.va.gov/*

Veterans Can Get Extra Points on Their Federal Application Packages

www.fedshirevets.gov

For competitive or direct hire federal positions, veterans will receive extra points on their federal applications based on their military service.

5 points - Veterans Recruitment Appointment (VRA) (Formerly, Veterans Readjustment Appointment)
What it provides: VRA allows appointment of eligible veterans up to GS-11 or equivalent. Veterans are hired under excepted appointments to positions that are otherwise in the competitive service. After the individual satisfactorily completes two years of service, the veteran must be converted noncompetitively to a career or career-conditional appointment.

10 points - 30 Percent or More Disabled Veterans
What it provides: This authority enables a hiring manager to appoint an eligible candidate to any position for which he or she is qualified, without competition. Unlike the VRA, there is no grade-level limitation. Initial appointments are time limited, lasting more than 60 days; however, the manager can noncompetitively convert the individual to permanent status at any time during the time-limited appointment.

This authority applies to disabled veterans who were retired from active military service with a disability rating of 30 percent or more, and disabled veterans rated by the Department of Veterans Affairs (VA) within the preceding year as having a compensable service-connected disability of 30 percent or more.

10 points - Veterans Employment Opportunity Act of 1998 (VEOA)
What it provides: This flexibility gives eligible veterans access to jobs that otherwise only would have been available to status employees. In VEOA appointments, veterans are not accorded preference as a factor, but they are allowed to compete for job opportunities that are not offered to other external candidates. A VEOA eligible who is selected will be given a career or career-conditional appointment.

For more information about the Workforce Recruitment Program (WRP), visit http://mycareeratva.va.gov/Careerpath/Internships/Pages/WorkforceRecruitmentProgram.aspx

Additional Tips for Veteran Students on the Ten Steps to a Federal Job®

Step 1. Research Federal Student Programs (for Veterans)

Check out the following programs that may help you get an entrance into the federal government either by internship or apprenticeship:

- NAVSEA Wounded Warrior Internship Programs:
  www.navsea.navy.mil/Organization/WoundedWarriors.aspx

- Department of Homeland Security, Wounded Warrior Program:
  www.dhs.gov/wounded-warrior-program

- Department of Veterans Affairs (VA):
  VA Acquisition Academy – The Acquisition Internship School:
  www.acquisitionacademy.va.gov/schools/internship/

- U.S. Department of Veterans Affairs VetSuccess:
  Information about military skills translators, resources, and job fairs for Wounded Warriors: *www.vetsuccess.va.gov/*

Step 2. Network

It's possible for veterans to get hired directly by a supervisor. The Veterans Recruitment Act (VRA) offers special hiring programs for retiring and separating military (disabled or non-disabled). VRA gives supervisors the authority to make direct hires in the case of veterans, but be aware that even under direct hiring, the jobseeker must submit an application. The best opportunity for a direct hire is a military job fair. If you can find a military job fair where agencies are present, it is possible that you could be given a job offer on the spot! You must be well-prepared with an internship or USAJOBS resume, like the samples in this book. Do you know a supervisor at an agency or a military base? You can also contact them directly to ask about possible job openings that they may have now or in the near future.

Step 3. Find Your Agency, Job Title, and Grade

When choosing your agency and job title, you will need to translate your military skills into language appropriate for government and private sector jobs. You will need to blend the titles of your matching positions from your recent military career, plus your college major and determine what federal job titles will be right for you. You can find a match to your military MOS to the OPM Classification Standards at *www.dllr.state.md.us/mil2fedjobs/*.

MILITARY SERVICE MEMBERS AND VETERANS

› Identify federal jobs related to your military occupation

› Find out about the federal job characteristics, such as duties, pay grade and qualifications

› Search USAJOBS for vacancies

SEARCH BY MILITARY OCCUPATION

LEARN ABOUT FEDERAL JOBS

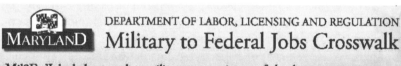

MARYLAND | DEPARTMENT OF LABOR, LICENSING AND REGULATION
Military to Federal Jobs Crosswalk

Mil2FedJobs helps translate military occupations to federal jobs. Use the search features below to get started.

SERVICE MEMBER/VETERAN SEARCH

To find out what federal jobs are related to specific military occupations, use the following steps:

Step 1. Select the Service and the Personnel Category
Service:

○ Army ○ Navy ○ Air Force ○ Marine Corps ○ Coast Guard

Personnel Category:

○ Officer ○ Warrant Officer ○ Enlisted

Step 2. Select a Military Occupation
Military Occupation Code:
-- Choose a Code --
- or -
Military Occupation Title:
-- Choose a Title --

Step 4. Finding The Right Positions For You

Many student veterans apply for internships or positions with military services as a civilian or with Department of Defense (DoD) agencies in order to continue a military or defense-focused career path.

Alternatively, if you are seeking a position outside of DoD or the military, look at other agencies where you can use your skills and college education. There are over 200 agencies in the federal government. Many of these share your mission to support veterans but in ways you have not thought of yet. Be flexible and look for positions throughout the federal government.

Step 5. Analyzing Federal Jobs For You

As a veteran, you receive 5 points for your military service or 10 points if you are a disabled veteran with 30% disability or more. So, if you achieve the level of Best Qualified in the Category Rating review system, you will receive an additional 5 or 10 points for a permanent Civil Service position. *In order to GET your points, your resume has to be Qualified for a position.* Therefore, selecting the vacancy announcements, position titles, and grade levels will be important. Make sure you have the education, qualifications, and Specialized Experience for the position. If your federal resume is well written and you are qualified for the position, your additional veteran's preference points will help you get Best Qualified and referred to a supervisor

Step 6. Federal Resume Writing

See Jeremy Denton's Sample Student Veteran USAJOBS Federal Resume and Internship Resume. (See Jeremy's case resume on page 131.)

Jeremy wants to move away from aviation and helicopters in his next career, so the strategy for writing his federal resume was to feature his transferrable skills: critical thinking, team leadership, safety, and operations. His bachelors degree in Government and Public Policy supported his objective to move into analysis of public programs. These transferrable skills matched his target announcement for Program Analyst. By adding his accomplishments, he proves that he is responsible, dedicated to his mission, and capable of being a team leader and analyst in mission critical situations.

Keep in mind that a veteran must receive a score of at least 70, or be Minimally Qualified, in order take advantage of the 5- or 10-point preference program. Your federal resume must match the announcement in terms of specialized experience and qualifications to demonstrate that you have the minimum qualifications.

Here are examples of weak and good work experience sections for a veteran student:

> *Not enough details in the work experience:*
> 10/2004-01/2008, **HELICOPTER CREW CHIEF**; E-5, Sgt, 3rd Marine Air Wing, Marine Corps Air Station Miramar, San Diego, CA
>
> - TEAM LEAD / FLIGHT CREW MEMBER: Planned, organized, led, and performed maintenance on helicopters, including during Operation Iraqi Freedom. Performed daily inspections on assigned aircraft; assisted in preflight inspections performing final checks; monitored aircraft performance during flight; assisted as a lookout and advised pilot of obstacles and other aircraft. Analyzed weight, mission, cargo and prepared aircraft for maximum defense. Utilized evaluative and technical skills in operating aircraft mounted weapons systems

Good description of work experience:
10/2004-01/2008
HELICOPTER CREW CHIEF; E-5, Sgt, 3rd Marine Air Wing, Marine Corps Air Station Miramar, San Diego, CA

- TEAM LEAD / FLIGHT CREW MEMBER: Planned, organized, led, and performed maintenance on CH-53E Super Stallion helicopters, including during Operation Iraqi Freedom. Supported more than 2,000 sorties in several major campaigns

- SCHEDULING AND COORDINATION: Performed daily inspections on assigned aircraft; assisted in preflight inspections performing final checks; monitored aircraft performance during flight; assisted as a lookout and advised pilot of obstacles and other aircraft

- KEY ACCOMPLISHMENTS: LOGGED 1,200 flight hours WITHOUT A SINGLE LOSS OF LIFE OR AIRCRAFT during two tours in Iraq and in the United States, including during combat conditions, armed interdictions, border patrolling, and medical evacuations of military and civilians

Step 7. KSAs, Questionnaires, and Cover Letters

Check out the resume sample on page 137 showing how Brandon Billings demonstrates KSAs in the Work Experience section of the resume with keywords and description for a career as E-5, USCG in Maritime Security, Law Enforcement, Investigation, and Communication.

Brandon's federal resume focuses on skills and experiences that demonstrate the Knowledge, Skills, and Abilities required for the targeted position. Brandon's military experience was as an E-5, USCG in Maritime Security, Law Enforcement, Investigation, and Communication. He wanted to continue his career in security, law enforcement, and investigations with his new bachelors degree in Homeland Security Studies. The resume features his skills that support his new civilian target position in homeland security, law enforcement, and investigations. The resume also highlights Brandon's degree, especially the courses and projects in: Transportation Security, Risk Analysis, and Emergency Management.

Step 8. Submit Your Application

Make sure you know which documents must be submitted for veterans preference and eligibility programs. Upload your documents well before any deadline.

Transcripts must be added into your USAJOBS account so that you can qualify for positions based on education. You can scan your original transcripts into the USAJOBS account.

All Veterans are required to submit a DD-214, Military Discharge (Member Copy 4). Veterans claiming 10 Point Preference must additionally submit a completed SF-15 and the supporting documents outlined on the SF-15. *www.opm.gov/forms/pdf_fill/SF15.pdf*

Application of Veterans Preference: The Category Rating Method protects the rights of veterans by placing them ahead of non-preference eligible applicants within each category. Be aware that you must demonstrate in your resume that you are at least Minimally Qualified to be considered "preference eligible." Preference eligibles who have a compensable service-connected disability of at least 10 percent must be listed in the highest quality category, except for scientific or professional positions at the GS-9 grade level or higher. In most cases, a selecting official may make selections from the highest quality category (Best Qualified).

For information on entitlement see *www.fedshirevets.gov/job/vetpref/index.aspx*.

Step 9. Track and Follow Up

Veterans can track and follow up on USAJOBS applications in the same way as all other students and federal job applicants. When you email a human resources specialist regarding a position or application, be sure to add to the subject line that you are a veteran (5- or 10-point veteran), along with your name to help improve the understanding of your hiring situation and programs.

Step 10. Interview for a Federal Job

In order to prepare for a behavior-based interview, write about your military leadership, teamwork, training, critical thinking, and accomplishments ahead of time. Write them down and prepare to talk about them in terms of the skills that could be used in that position. Be sensitive in practicing and preparing your accomplishments. It's good to tell stories that are relevant with enough details to give meaning. Many veteran accomplishments may have to do with operations that will not be relevant here in a peaceful country. Edit your accomplishments and make sure they are relevant for the agency's mission; support the position knowledge, skills, and abilities; and demonstrate your dedication to achieving your past and future objectives.

Sample Federal Resumes and Cover Letters

Sample Successful Resumes

Sample Cover Letters

Student Veterans Resumes

ANNE CRANE -- HIRED -- FIRST APPLICATION SUBMITTED!
Health Insurance Specialist, GS-11/12
Center for Medicare & Medicaid Services
1 Year of PhD studies in Counseling Psychology
MS, Applied Psychology
BA, English Literature

USAJOBS Upload Format

Anne Crane

1136 Canton Avenue
Baltimore, MD 21230
Phone: 240-444-4444
Email: anne.crane@gmail.com

Job Number: HHS-CMS-DE/MP-12-77777
Position: Health Insurance Specialist (GS-0107)
Grade: GS 09-12

Objective: To obtain a position in healthcare

Summary of Skills:

Statistical Analysis

Data entry and analysis using SPSS, SAS, and Excel;
Data visualization techniques (graphs, charts, scatterplots, structural equation modeling);
Matrix/Linear Algebra methods;
ANOVA, MANOVA, Correlation, Linear Regression, Multiple Regression, Chi Square, Chronbach's Alpha, post hoc assessments, and various other methodologies;
Moderating and mediating variables

Feature the keywords from the announcement.

Research Analysis

Planning and design of research studies on social media, women's healthcare, and healthcare training; budget design and analysis; facilitating data collection and administration of assessment tools; analysis of findings and interpretation of results; presentation of results at conferences; powerpoint presentations and research paper publications

Healthcare

Provided mental healthcare to elementary and middle school children and their families in Baltimore City; provided families on Medicaid information and resources for affordable healthcare; research presentation on healthcare and harmful practices towards women in Nigeria; created proposal for college mental health outreach program targeting Asia Americans and international students; assisted retirees on transitioning to Medicare from university healthcare benefits; helped navigate Baltimore City families, while working as counselor in inner city school, to affordable healthcare services and discussed utilizing Medicaid

Computer Skills:
SPSS, SAS, Peopleware Pro, Oculus, RefWorks, Opus, Global Link
Word, Adobe-Acrobat, Excel, Access, PowerPoint, Pagemaker

Software skills are listed close to the top.

Education:
1 year of PhD studies in Counseling Psychology
September 2011-May 2012
University of Pennsylvania, Philadelphia, PA
Overall GPA: 3.91/4.0

M.S. in Applied Psychology, 2011
University of Baltimore, Baltimore, MD
Overall GPA: 3.87/4.0

B.A. in English Literature,2007
University of Towson, Towson, MD
Overall GPA: 3.54/4.0

Honors:
Cum Laude, Psy Chi (National Psychology Honor Society), Dean's List

Related Coursework:

List relevant courses.

Intermediate Statistics, Univariate Statistics, Multivariate Statistics, Research Methods I and II, Professional Writing and Communication, Ethics and Law, Law and Society, Human Development, Multicultural Counseling, Tests and Assessments, Human Development Across the Lifespan, Biological Basis of Behavior (Neuropschology), Psychopathology and Diagnosis, Psychological Development, Adolescent Development

Major Papers and Research:

Major research papers and projects are detailed.

Crane, A., CWSI, Walters, T., Lieberman, A., Trenton, S., & Siu, L. (2012). Harmful Practices: Violence Against Women in Nigeria. Paper to be presented at symposium at the 30th International Congress of Psychology. 1st author and member of team creating presentation for international conference. Collaborated with Nigerian NGO in order to present their data on violence against women and proposed legislation. Created powerpoint for presentation and prepped teammates for presentation in South Africa in July, 2012. Interpreted the data and determined that findings suggest harmful practices such as female genital mutilation are still in existence in Nigeria. Findings also show that the government although these practices exist, members of the community as well as governmental officials are reluctant to discuss the issue.

Did you design a project?

Crane, A. Preston, C., & Frame, S. (2011). Individuals' Impressions: the Effect of Gossip and Gender on Personality Disorders. Poster presented at 23rd Annual Association for Psychological Science Convention (May 2011). Designed and administered study on human behavior, gossip, and social media. Created methodology for study and created assessment tool. Administered assessment tool to subjects. Gathered consent from subjects and university, in the form of consent forms and IRB. Used 2-way ANOVA to analyze data in SPSS. Found that female subjects were more likely to view females poorly due to negative gossip, rather than males. Presented findings at Association of Psychological Science annual conference in Washington, DC (July 2011).

Healthcare Article Critques. Evaluated and critiqued 3 current journal articles on healthcare relating to Asian Americans, multicultural competency, and the effect of racial matching on the patient's perception of quality care. Wrote papers regarding critique of the articles' methodology, sampling method, and assessments. Presented critiques to class (November 2011).

Self-Care Brochure: Designed brochure for healthcare professionals on the importance of self-care. Presented coping strategies such as, meditation, deep breathing, and counseling (December 2011).

University Suicide Prevention Program: Created proposal and design of a suicide prevention program. Outreach focused on Asian Americans students and other minorities. Designed program in terms of outreach procedures, workshops, and presentations. Outreach including clubs on campus, sports teams, Greek life, and incoming freshman. Workshops included role-playing, information on additional services, and warning signs. Presented proposal to university students (October 2011).

Presentation on the Millon Clinical Multiaxial Inventory III assessment tool (May 2012). Discussed evolution of the assessment tool. Evaluated assessment tool and created visual aid of pros and cons. Found that although the Millon has high validity, it has an issue with response bias. Assessed which populations the Millon is appropriate for.

Work Experience:

Benefits Assistant (contracted employee)   **September 2012 – Present**
Johns Hopkins University
1101 E 3rd St., Baltimore, MD 21218   *$16.50/hour*
Supervisor: Craig Raine   *40 Hours/Week*
    Duties: Worked with retirees and current employees to help them submit necessary paperwork and information for healthcare benefits. Assisted retirees on their transition from JHU health insurance to Medicare/Medicaid.

Graduate and Research Assistant   **September 2011 – May 2012**
Lehigh University
111 Research Drive, Bethlehem, PA 18015   *$7,500 stipend*
Supervisor: Dr. Carlotta Regent   *20 Hours/Week*
    Duties: Conducted literature reviews and organized articles for future research using RefWorks. Collected and analyzed previous relevant research for a proposal of funding on a study about women graduate students in healthcare professions. Evaluated proposed research studies for technical feasibility and methodology. Edited and prepared articles and book chapters for publications. Analyzed statistical data using SPSS and created tables and graphs. Researched assessment tools for current studies. Worked in collaboration with a team on researching and analyzing previous relevant research findings, including implications, issues, and future directions.

Research Assistant   **September 2010 – May 2011**
University of Baltimore
1420 N. Charles Street, Baltimore, MD 21201   *Not paid*
Supervisor: Dr. Barnard Wilth   *15 Hours/Week*
    Duties: Conducted literature reviews and researched articles for proposal of research study regarding mental healthcare required due to the protean career. Analyzed previous relevant research and results. Assisted with conducting studies on the impact of careers on mental health. Collected and entered data in SPSS. Facilitated collection of data and administration of tests and assessment tools. Researched assessment tools and measures for future study. Analyzed various factors such as, time needed, price of assessment tools, and labor to create budget for future research study.

Month and year is mandatory.
Salary is optional.
Hours per week: mandatory

Psychology Extern

September 2010 – May 2011

University of Maryland School Mental Health Program
701 W. Pratt St., 4th FL, Baltimore, MD 21201

Not paid

Supervisor: Moses Muhammed, MSW

20 Hours/Week

> Duties: Worked as a mental health therapist in a Baltimore City public Elementary/Middle School. Administered intakes to potential clients. Provided confidential individual and group counseling to clients and families on Medicaid and Medicare. Evaluated students and provided DSM diagnoses. Assisted families in finding appropriate healthcare options in the area based on their insurance needs. Visited clients' homes in order to assess their living and family environment. Provided community outreach to families and educated parents additional services in the area, such as, healthcare options and parenting classes. Interpreted national and state laws, such as HIPPA, as well as ethics codes, in order to provide the best services to clients. Evaluated by supervisor and received the highest evaluation marks possible.

United Nations NGO Delegate

October 2011 – May 2012

Center for Women's Studies and Intervention
Abuja, Nigeria

Not paid

Supervisor: Dr. Wilsonian Tambuwal

15 Hours/Week

> Duties: Acted as the personal representative for the CWSI NGO at the UN and UN related events, including: video phone calls and presentations, meetings, and conferences. Interacted with executive officers and high ranking US and foreign government officials in order to provide information about the NGO's mission to assist women in Nigeria with their healthcare needs and the proposal for new legislation and healthcare policy. Presented to the Lehigh University board of directors about harmful practices, such as female genital mutilation, in Nigeria. Attended UN briefings once a month on behalf of the NGO for the Center for Women's Studies and Intervention (CWSI). Advocated and networked for the NGO at UN events. Provided briefings to the NGO about relevant information from UN events. Worked in collaboration with the NGO to help submit research on harmful traditional practices in Nigeria to the International Congress of Psychology conference in South Africa (July 2012). Presentation involved the proposal of change in legislation and the technical feasibility, economic viability, and impact on Nigeria.

ANNE CRANE -- HIRED -- FIRST APPLICATION SUBMITTED!
Health Insurance Specialist, GS-11/12
Center for Medicare & Medicaid Services
1 Year of PhD studies in Counseling Psychology
MS, Applied Psychology
BA, English Literature

Harvard Format

The Harvard Format has headings on the left in a separate column.

Anne Crane

1136 Canton Avenue
Baltimore, MD 21230
Phone: 240-444-4444
Email: anne.crane@gmail.com

OBJECTIVE: **Public Health Statistician**

EDUCATION: **UNIVERSITY OF PENNSYLVANIA, Ph.D. Candidate, Counseling Psychology, Expected May 2014**
September 2011 to present

Related Coursework:
Intermediate Statistics, Univariate Statistics, Multivariate Statistics, Research Methods I and II, Professional Writing and Communication, Ethics and Law, Law and Society, Human Development, Multicultural Counseling, Tests and Assessments, Human Development Across the Lifespan, Biological Basis of Behavior (Neuropsychology), Psychopathology and Diagnosis, Psychological Development, Adolescent Development

UNIVERSITY OF BALTIMORE, M.S., Applied Psychology, 2011
UNIVERSITY OF TOWSON, B.A., English Literature, 2007
Honors: Cum Laude, Psy Chi, Dean's List

Adding courses to a private sector resume is a good idea.

MAJOR PAPERS AND RESEARCH:

Adding research papers and projects to a private industry resume is important. Projects clearly demonstrate statistical skills.

Crane, A., CWSI, Walters, T., Lieberman, A., Trenton, S., & Siu, L. (2012). *Harmful Practices: Violence Against Women in Nigeria.* Paper to be presented at symposium at the 30th International Congress of Psychology. 1st author and member of team creating presentation for international conference.

Crane, A. Preston, C., & Frame, S. (2011). *Individuals' Impressions: the Effect of Gossip and Gender on Personality Disorders.* **Poster presented at 23rd Annual Association for Psychological Science Convention (May 2011).** Designed and administered study on human behavior, gossip, and social media. Created methodology for study and created assessment tool. Administered assessment tool to subjects. Gathered consent from subjects and university, in the form of consent forms and IRB.

Healthcare Article Critiques. Evaluated and critiqued 3 current journal articles on healthcare relating to Asian Americans, multicultural competency, and the effect of racial matching on the patient's perception of quality care.

Self-Care Brochure: Designed brochure for healthcare professionals on the importance of self-care. Presented coping strategies such as meditation, deep breathing, and counseling (December 2011).

University Suicide Prevention Program: Created proposal and design of a suicide prevention program. Outreach focused on Asian American students and other minorities (October 2011).

Presentation on the Millon Clinical Multiaxial Inventory III assessment tool (May 2012). Discussed evolution of the assessment tool. Evaluated assessment tool and created visual aid of pros and cons.

WORK EXPERIENCE:

JOHNS HOPKINS UNIVERSITY, Baltimore, MD   Sept. 2012 to present
Benefits Assistant - Worked with retirees and current employees to help them submit necessary paperwork and information for healthcare benefits.

LEHIGH UNIVERSITY, Bethlehem, PA   Sept. 2011 - May 2012
Graduate and Research Assistant - Conducted literature reviews and organized articles for future research using RefWorks. Collected and analyzed relevant research for a study about women graduate students in healthcare professions.

UNIVERSITY OF BALTIMORE, Baltimore, MD   Sept. 2010 – May 2011
Research Assistant - Conducted literature reviews and researched articles for proposal of research study regarding mental healthcare required due to the protean career. Analyzed previous relevant research and results. Assisted with conducting studies on the impact of careers on mental health. Collected and entered data in SPSS.

UNIVERSITY OF MARYLAND SCHOOL OF MENTAL HEALTH Sept. 2010 – May 2011
Psychology Extern - Worked as a mental health therapist in a Baltimore City public Elementary/Middle School. Administered intakes to potential clients. Provided confidential individual and group counseling to clients and families on Medicaid and Medicare.

UNITED NATIONS, Abuja, Nigeria   Oct. 2011 – May 2012
Center for Women's Studies and Intervention
NGO Delegate - Acted as the personal representative for the CWSI NGO at the UN and UN related events. Provided briefings to the NGO from UN events (July 2012).

TECHNICAL SKILLS:

Clear list of highly-technical statistical software skills

Statistical Analysis
Data entry and analysis using SPSS, SAS, and Excel;
Data visualization techniques (graphs, charts, scatterplots, structural equation modeling);
Matrix/Linear Algebra methods; ANOVA, MANOVA, Correlation, Linear Regression, Multiple Regression, Chi Square, Chronbach's Alpha, post hoc assessments, and various other methodologies; Moderating and mediating variables

Research Analysis
Planning and design of research studies on social media, women's healthcare, and healthcare training; budget design and analysis; facilitating data collection and administration of assessment tools; analysis of findings and interpretation of results; presentation of results at conferences; PowerPoint presentations and publications

Healthcare
Provided mental healthcare to elementary and middle school children and their families in Baltimore City; provided families on Medicaid information and resources for affordable healthcare; researched presentation on healthcare and harmful practices towards women in Nigeria; created proposal for college mental health outreach program.

Computer Skills:
SPSS, SAS, Peopleware Pro, Oculus, RefWorks, Opus, Global Link
Word, Adobe-Acrobat, Excel, Access, PowerPoint, PageMaker

PHILIP SANG -- HIRED!
Mechanical Engineer, GS-9/12
U.S. Army Corps of Engineers
Masters in Aerospace Engineering
BS, Aerospace Engineering
BS, Mechanical Engineering

USAJOBS Upload Format

PHILIP W. SANG
111 Kahula Street • Honolulu, HI 96822
Mobile: 808-333-3333 • Email: psang11@gmail.com

GOAL: To utilize my education and passion for engineering disciplines and problem-solving to contribute to a team effort in planning and carrying out assignments.

LICENSURE AND CERTIFICATION
Engineering License Certification: Engineer-In Training: Mechanical Engineering, 10/2010, State of California

Licensure featured

COMPUTER PROFICIENCIES: Applications: Microsoft Office, AutoCAD 2010, Pro/Engineer, MathCAD, CAD/CAM with Numerical Control; Programming Languages: C++, MATlab 2010a

EDUCATION:

Start with Education since this is the most recent and relevant experience.

MASTER OF SCIENCE IN AEROSPACE ENGINEERING   08/2010-12/2011
University of Southern California (USC), Los Angeles, CA 90089
GPA: 3.33, 24 Total Semester Credits

Developed and honed skills in all phases of engineering projects. As part of teams and individually, designed, researched and developed solutions to engineering problems. Made engineering calculations, wrote specifications and selected and identified materials. Conducted testing and troubleshooting to assure design met needs. Observed, tracked and evaluated performance data and prepared reports on findings. Made recommendations for best designs, testing, operations and maintenance.

ACADEMIC DESIGN PROJECTS:

Post-graduate engineering projects described in technical detail. Very impressive and proves skill and experience.

- Next Generation Mobile Cloud Computing Technology: Member of team that designed device that could be used for mobile cloud computing; device had stronger processing power than a cell phone, but was more portable than a laptop. The project consisted of modifying and compromising between various available technologies to produce a design that would be functional, reliable and economical. Design consisted of cell phone that projected a laser keyboard onto any flat surface with glasses to serve as a visual display and gloves to interact with objects on the visual display; the entire system remotely connected to a desktop at home with strong computing power.

- Dynamics of a Rotating Baseball: Lead programmer and numerical analysis assistant for five-person team that calculated the aerodynamic forces placed on a rotating baseball as it travels from the pitcher to the batter. Location of fastball pitch was determined, which determined the initial velocities and angles at which the pitch was thrown. Used MATlab code to simulate the movement of a different pitch with a different spin with the same initial angles.

➢ COURSEWORK: Dynamics of Incompressible Fluids, Engineering Analytical Methods, Engineering Analysis, Compressible Gas Dynamics, Advanced Mechanical Design, Project Controls- Planning and Scheduling, Systems Architecting, Combustion Chemistry and Physics, Principles of Combustion, Advanced Dynamics

Courses listed in the resume.

BACHELOR OF SCIENCE, AEROSPACE ENGINEERING   05/2010
BACHELOR OF SCIENCE, MECHANICAL ENGINEERING
Illinois Institute of Technology (IIT), Chicago, IL 60616
GPA: 3.56 out of 4.00, 128 Total Semester Credits
Supervisor: Candace Worth, Ph.D., Phone: 312-333-3333, May contact

Graduated Cum Laude, 05/2010

Team lead and
project details
with technical
descriptions.

ACADEMIC DESIGN PROJECTS:

- Smoke Wire Flow Visualization Over Car Models: Team leader for project to determine which car design reduced aerodynamic drag the most. Took pictures of streamlines exposed by oil on a heat wire producing smoke trails in the airflow of a wind tunnel. Photos showed which car models experienced flow separation or the extent of the flow separation, the leading cause of aerodynamic drag. Then used photos to determine which car design was best suited for the tested wind speeds.

- Large-Scale Building Solar Air Conditioning System: As member of six-person team, served as lead for system design and CAD design, and numerical analysis assistant. Researched and designed solar-powered air-conditioning system. The final design used parabolic mirrors that would focus the sun's rays to one point, heating up the molten salt that is then stored in a large silo, capable of holding enough energy to power the system overnight. The salt would heat liquid ammonia into a gas that runs through a heat exchanger with air, which cools the air during summer. During winter, the heat exchanger would run in reverse to warm the facility. The thermodynamic equations were placed into an energy equation solver that solved the unknown parameters through guess and check.

- Light Sport Aircraft Automobile: On four-person team, served as lead for numerical analysis and optimization and design analysis assistant. Designed vehicle that would be capable of driving on any road in the U.S. and be able to fly while carrying at least two passengers. Followed commercial vehicle regulations, which constrained aircraft size and the size of control surfaces, which meant folding the wings. Set maximum allowable flight parameters to match that of a light sport aircraft pilot license.

- Automatic Glove Dispenser: Served as CAD design, structural load analysis and design analysis lead for six-person team. Designed and produced alpha prototype of an automatic glove dispenser. Researched, developed, produced and tested various mockups, including materials selection; settled on a top-loading glove dispenser that would utilize gravity to load gloves into a tray, which would allow users to slide their hands into the gloves without touching the outside of the gloves, keeping the gloves sterile.

- ➤ RELEVANT COURSEWORK: Calculus: Multi-variable, Vector and Differential Equations; Statics; Dynamics; Aircraft and Spacecraft Dynamics; Aerodynamics of Aerospace Vehicles; Fluid Mechanics; Compressible Flow; Aerospace Propulsion; Thermodynamics; Applied Thermodynamics (Refrigeration and Heaters); Design of Thermal Systems; Engineering Materials and Design; Analysis of Aerostructures; Systems Analysis and Control; Engineering Measurements; Drafting
Physics: Mechanical, Electrical, and Modern; CAD/CAM with Numerical Control, Spacecraft and Aircraft Mechanics; Design of Mechanical Systems; Heat and Mass Transfer; Finite Element Methods in Engineering; Design of Aerospace Vehicles I (Fixed Wing Aircraft Design Practices); Design of Aerospace Vehicles II (Design of Space Launch Vehicles and Satellites).

WORK EXPERIENCE:

ENGINEERING TECHNICIAN (Intern), GS-0802-05   **05/2011-08/2011**
United States Coast Guard, Civil Engineering Unit, Honolulu, HI 96850
Hours/week: 40
Supervisor: Neal Kamona, Phone: 808-444-4444, May contact

Month and year and hours per week worked are required to prove One Year Specialiazed Experience.

- APPLIED ENGINEERING PRINCIPLES AND CONCEPT KNOWLEDGE to evaluate designs for $5M C-130 Hercules rinse rack that complied with military regulations and FAA height restrictions. Researched concepts that incorporated a reverse-osmosis water-filtration system to reclaim used water to reduce water usage and that required minimal maintenance over system lifetime. Reviewed plans, manuals, instruction books, technical standards, guides and reports to identify problem areas and assess feasibility. Performed cost analysis on potential rinse rack positions and variety of existing rinse rack systems.

- COMMUNICATED ORALLY AND IN WRITING. Worked closely with engineers, senior and support staff and stakeholders. Coordinated meetings with contracting companies regarding site preparation for C-130 rinse rack at the local air station. Contacted State of Hawai'i officials to obtain as-built drawings for a floating dock project that was slated to moor a pair of 100-foot Coast Guard cutters; coordinated site visits to assess ocean swell conditions at the State of Hawai'i floating dock and assessed the dock's performance.

Floating dock story was used in the job interview.

- USED TECHNICAL SKILLS to update and maintain engineering drawing database by filing as-built, engineering and surveying drawings with proper descriptions of each drawing.

ENGINEERING TECHNICIAN, GS-0802-05   **05/2010-09/2010**
United States Coast Guard, Base Support Unit, San Pedro, CA 90731
Hours/week: 40
Supervisor: Len Roses, Phone: 310-555-5555, May not contact

It's OK to say "may not contact" supervisor.

- DEMONSTRATED ENGINEERING KNOWLEDGE AND SKILL in consulting with Civil Engineering Unit Oakland (CEU Oakland) and updating drawing database; introduced the office to the system widely used throughout the Coast Guard, replacing the previous method, which used a collection of on hand copies of drawings obtained from CEU Oakland. Developed drawings for base projects, including a living quarters renovation and office space expansion.

ALL CAPS ARE KEYWORDS from KSAs or Specialiazed Experience.

ENGINEERING TECHNICIAN, GS-0802-04   06/2009-08/2009
United States Coast Guard- Civil Engineering Unit
Honolulu, HI 96850
Hours/week: 40
Supervisor: Neal Kamona, Phone: 808-555-5555, May contact

- COMMUNICATED ORALLY AND IN WRITING. Performed engineering site visits with design team leader, lead mechanical engineer and lead electrical engineer on installing a new wind turbine system to improve base security when power is cut off and the base needs to be locked down. Went on site visits to improve and maintain jet fuel pumping station holding tanks and pipes used to move the fuel.

Communicating orally and in writing is a typical KSA for federal jobs.

- DEMONSTRATED knowledge of professional engineering concepts, principles and practices in engineering development of solar water heating system for Coast Guard locker room under the guidance of the lead mechanical engineer. Performed entire project from design of the system to the system's parts.

- UTILIZED ORGANIZATIONAL SKILLS and knowledge of AutoCAD 2010 to electronically consolidate all current utility drawings of the base into one master drawing that accurately identified the correct position of any utility seen and unseen on the air station.

PROFESSIONAL REFERENCES

Neal Kamona, Design Team Leader, US Coast Guard - Civil Engineering Unit Honolulu
300 Ala Moana Blvd 8-134, Honolulu, HI 96850
Phone Number: 808-888-8888; Email:

Gail Goingo, Lead Architect, US Coast Guard - Civil Engineering Unit Honolulu
300 Ala Moana Blvd 8-134, Honolulu, HI 96850
Phone Number: 808-555-5555; Email:

PHILIP SANG -- HIRED!
Mechanical Engineer, GS-9/12
U.S. Army Corps of Engineers
Masters in Aerospace Engineering
BS, Aerospace Engineering
BS, Mechanical Engineering

Traditional Paper Format: 2-Page Private Industry Resume

PHILIP W. SANG

111 Kahula Street • Honolulu, HI 96822
Mobile: 808-333-3333 • Email: psang11@gmail.com

OBJECTIVE:
Aerospace Engineer … Mechanical Engineer … Project Manager … Test Manager

> The objective can change depending on the target position.

LICENSURE AND CERTIFICATION
Engineering License Certification: Engineer-In Training: Mechanical Engineering, 10/2010, State of California

> Licenses and certifications should go first on a resume.

COMPUTER PROFICIENCIES
Applications: Microsoft Office, AutoCAD 2010, Pro/Engineer, MathCAD, CAD/CAM with Numerical Control; Programming Languages: C++, MATlab 2010a

> Technical skills must be easy to find by the HR recruiter.

EDUCATION

MASTER OF SCIENCE IN AEROSPACE ENGINEERING   08/2010-12/2011
University of Southern California (USC), Los Angeles, CA; GPA: 3.33

Developed and honed skills in all phases of engineering projects. As part of teams and individually, designed, researched and developed solutions to engineering problems. Made engineering calculations, wrote specifications and selected and identified materials. Conducted testing and troubleshooting to assure design met needs. Observed, tracked and evaluated performance data and prepared reports on findings. Made recommendations for best designs, testing, operations and maintenance.

ACADEMIC DESIGN PROJECTS:
- Next Generation Mobile Cloud Computing Technology: Member of team that designed device that could be used for mobile cloud computing; device had stronger processing power than a cell phone, but was more portable than a laptop.

- Dynamics of a Rotating Baseball: Lead programmer and numerical analysis assistant for five-person team that calculated the aerodynamic forces placed on a rotating baseball as it travels from the pitcher to the batter. Used MATlab code to simulate the movement of a different pitch with a different spin with the same initial angles.

BACHELOR OF SCIENCE, AEROSPACE ENGINEERING   05/2010
BACHELOR OF SCIENCE, MECHANICAL ENGINEERING
Graduated Cum Laude
Illinois Institute of Technology (IIT), Chicago, IL
GPA: 3.56 out of 4.00, 128 Total Semester Credits

> Titles of projects and short descriptions make the resume interesting for the HR recruiter and hiring manager. This can help you get an interview.

ACADEMIC DESIGN PROJECTS:
- Smoke Wire Flow Visualization Over Car Models: Team leader for project to determine which car design reduced aerodynamic drag the most.

Bullet format for the duties is preferred
by private industry HR recruiters.

- <u>Large-Scale Building Solar Air Conditioning System:</u> As member of six-person team, served as lead for system design and CAD design, and numerical analysis assistant. Researched and designed solar-powered air-conditioning system.

- <u>Light Sport Aircraft Automobile:</u> On four-person team, served as lead for numerical analysis and optimization and design analysis assistant. Designed vehicle that would be capable of driving on any road in the U.S. and be able to fly while carrying at least two passengers.

- <u>Automatic Glove Dispenser:</u> Served as CAD design, structural load analysis and design analysis lead for six-person team. Designed alpha prototype of an automatic glove dispenser.

ENGINEERING TECHNICIAN (Intern), GS-0802-05   **05/2011-08/2011**
United States Coast Guard, Civil Engineering Unit, Honolulu, HI; Hours/week: 40
- Evaluated designs for $5M C-130 Hercules rinse rack that complied with military regulations and FAA height restrictions.
- Researched concepts that incorporated a reverse-osmosis water-filtration system to reclaim used water to reduce water usage and that required minimal maintenance over system lifetime.
- Worked closely with engineers, senior and support staff and stakeholders.
- Coordinated meetings with contracting companies regarding site preparation for C-130 rinse rack at the local air station. Contacted State of Hawai'i officials to obtain as-built drawings for a floating dock project that was slated to moor a pair of 100-foot Coast Guard cutters.
- Coordinated site visits to assess ocean swell conditions at the State of Hawai'i floating dock and assessed the dock's performance.
- Updated and maintained engineering drawing database by filing as-built, engineering and surveying drawings with proper descriptions of each drawing.

ENGINEERING TECHNICIAN, GS-0802-05   **05/2010-09/2010**
United States Coast Guard, Base Support Unit, San Pedro, CA; Hours/week: 40

- Consulted with Civil Engineering Unit Oakland (CEU Oakland) and updating drawing database.
- Introduced the office to the system widely used throughout the Coast Guard, replacing the previous method, which used a collection of copies of drawings obtained from CEU Oakland.
- Developed drawings for base projects, including a living quarters renovation and office space expansion.

ENGINEERING TECHNICIAN, GS-0802-04   06/2009-08/2009
United States Coast Guard- Civil Engineering Unit, Honolulu, HI; Hours/week: 40

- Performed engineering site visits with design team leader, lead mechanical engineer and lead electrical engineer on installing a new wind turbine system to improve base security when power is cut off and the base needs to be locked down.
- Managed engineering project to develop a solar water heating system for Coast Guard locker room under the guidance of the lead mechanical engineer. Performed entire project from design of the system to the system's parts.
- Utilized AutoCAD 2010 to electronically consolidate all current utility drawings of the base into one master drawing that accurately identified the correct position of any utility seen and unseen on the air station.

RACHEL BELL -- HIRED!
Student Trainee, New Media Specialist (HR),
GS-1099-7/9

    BA, English and Linguistics (double major)

USAJOBS Upload Format

RACHEL BELL
1234 Doorpost Rd
College Park, MD 20741
Cell: 443-333-3333
Email: rachelbell@email.com

PROFILE: Dynamic, self-driven, and collaborative Human Resources Management student graduating with a Master's of Science (MS) degree in May 2012. Exceptional interpersonal, customer relations, organizational, and oral and written communication skills. Experience providing program and administrative support for projects and programs. Goal oriented, high energy individual with excellent attention to detail. Proven analytical and research skills; ability to identify significant factors, gather pertinent data, and recognize solutions. Personable and responsible; cooperative and courteous to coworkers and customers. Polished, professional presentation.

EDUCATION:

Enrolled in Masters of Science (MS) program; Human Resource Management; Strayer University; Washington, DC; completed 9 quarter hours out of 54 total; anticipated graduation date, 05/2012; GPA: 3.5/4.0.

- WROTE MAJOR PAPER ON HUMAN RESOURCES: Successfully drafted and submitted a major paper utilizing human resources theory and management practices to explore the strategic role of management of core functions—total rewards, talent management, organizational development, HR information systems, and employee and labor relations.

- LED TEAM PROJECT ON LEADERSHIP AND ORGANIZATIONAL BEHAVIOR: Led a 5-member team on a complex research project analyzing the interaction of individual, group, and organizational dynamics that influence human behavior in organizations. Based on research findings, determined appropriate management approaches to foster a productive work environment.

- DELIVERED CONFERENCE PRESENTATION: Effectively used PowerPoint and oral delivery strategies to offer a presentation on human resource information systems at a nationwide conference. The presentation analyzed information technologies and systems used to maintain data relative to the human resource needs of a hypothetical organization.

Bachelor of Arts (BA); English and Linguistics (double major); University of Maryland; College Park, MD; May 2010; completed 129 semester hours; GPA: 3.67/4.0.

- Relevant Coursework: Digital Writing; Social Media Strategies; Marketing & Social Media; Managing the Digital Enterprise

- Key Project: Designed and regularly updated a "university life" blog garnering an audience both on and off-campus.

Study abroad program, University of Sheffield, Sheffield, England, 09/2008-06/2009. Diploma, Century High School, Eldersburg, MD, 2006.

WORK EXPERIENCE

05/2011–Present, Student Trainee, New Media Specialist (HR), GS-1099-07, U.S. Department of Energy, Washington, DC, 40 hours/week, Supervisor: George Warfield, 202-333-3333, may contact.

- PROJECT COORDINATION: Under supervision, work in a developmental capacity performing assignments and training in social media activities and strategies. Projects revolve around blogging, community development and management, social bookmarking, and commenting. Use judgment in selecting appropriate social media/new media tools and outlets. Efficiently work towards attaining social media outreach main objective to recruit top talent and brand the DOE as an "employer of choice."

- SOCIAL MEDIA INITIATIVES: Assist with the creation of a social media strategy to define programs that use social media marketing techniques to increase visibility, membership, and traffic across DOE employment brand. Monitor trends in social media tools and applications. Develop a DOEJobs Twitter account to alert the public of new job opportunities within the Department and other activities, such as job fairs.

- TEAMWORK AND COLLABORATION: Utilize analytical and strategic thinking skills to design and execute strategies through engagement of both internal and external DOE stakeholders. Coordinate efforts with the CIO and Office of Public Affairs to assure compliance with new media requirements. Maintain effective relations with staff in order to support strategies.

- ORAL COMMUNICATIONS AND CUSTOMER RELATIONS: Participate in staff conferences and contribute to program developments. Engage in proactive oral communications and establish and maintain effective working relationships. Interact with staff, management, and external stakeholders at all levels to facilitate communications. Brief supervisor on projects to ensure they meet primary goals and objectives.

- WRITTEN COMMUNICATIONS: Gather and present information on marketing and branding initiative to 18 other offices. Develop factual information, draft, and publish web 2.0 content for usage on social networking sites. Review for technical accuracy, proper use of accepted techniques and practices and overall compliance with instructions and organizational policy.

- KEY ACCOMPLISHMENTS: Initiated the roll-out of DOE/HC's Social Media presence by coordinating Social Media contributors across 18 Human Resources offices; creating and delivering presentations on the use of Social Media for recruitment; and designing and developing a high-visibility, high-traffic blog. My efforts substantially increased DOE's Social Media presence and garnered more than 5,000 "followers" on LinkedIn.

01/2010–05/2011, Employment Solutions Division Intern, Salary: $15/hour, U.S. Department of Energy, Washington, DC, 40 hours/week, Supervisor: George Warfield, 202-333-3333, may contact.

- On six-person Employment Solutions Division team, supported recruitment and retention initiatives for Office of Chief Human Capital Officer, with focus on Web 2.0 and marketing efforts.

- PROGRAM SUPPORT: Directly supported DOE recruiting programs, including intern, veteran and social media outreach. Collaborated on recruitment for 16 field offices and labs, working with local staff to schedule and organize recruitment events. Attended 8 recruitment events in fall 2010 to highlight DOE as an "Employer of Choice" to potential candidates. Scheduled meetings and provided administrative and programmatic support to leadership. Tracked inventory of recruiting and marketing materials for 18 offices.

- REPORTS / ADMINISTRATION: Collaborated on intern hire report, tracking DOE intern demographics for five years for goal-setting. Compiled and entered data on race, gender, schools, job series and retention, creating Excel spreadsheets and charts to measure effectiveness, efficacy and quality of human resources recruitment and retention initiatives. Final report identified hiring trends and quantified return on investment at recruiting events. Developed procedures and workflow for online recruitment efforts for social media, executing effort to integrate new media for communication and information. Researched and created list of potential college and university partners for social media and virtual efforts. Prepared partnership letters and monthly summer intern newsletters.

- KEY PROJECT: Edited the "Federal Intern Guide," a 110-page document on DOE internships for internal employees.

08/2007–07/2010, Facility Supervisor, Salary: $10.40/hour, Emerson Recreation Center, University of Maryland, College Park, MD, 7-12 hours/week, Supervisor: Ken Lance, 301-333-3333, may contact.

- CUSTOMER SERVICE: Maintained safe, welcoming fitness environment for students, faculty and administration. Answered questions, provided information, and resolved customer issues. Ensured staff adhered to customer service standards. Resolved discrepancies and reported thefts and disturbances to campus police. Exercised good judgment quickly during emergencies and provided medical assistance for injuries.

- STAFF SUPERVISION: Directed work of four staff members. Assigned tasks, checked work, and ensured completion. Interpreted and assured adherence to policies and procedures. Tracked and provided feedback on performance, including preparing disciplinary actions.

- FACILITY MANAGEMENT: Oversaw building operations, including maintenance, safety, and security. Checked regularly for spills, safety hazards, and proper equipment functioning. Tracked entry and departure of patrons.

- KEY ACCOMPLISHMENT: Coordinated logistics for large-scale event set-up/break-down, including the National YMCA Swimming Championships, with 4,000 attendees. Successfully ensured proper execution of all arrangements for attendees, participants, and judges.

EXTRACURRICULAR / VOLUNTEER ACTIVITIES:

- Beyond the Classroom, 09/2009–05/2010: Participated in yearlong Living and Learning Program exploring civic and social issues by taking part in issue-oriented classes, guest lectures, field trips and documentary and film series to develop leadership skills and civic engagement.

- Maryland Images, 03/2007–05/2009: Gave tours to prospective University of Maryland College Park students and their families, providing introductory information and history about the university. Maintained upbeat, positive attitude, providing information and tactfully answering difficult questions.

TRAINING / CERTIFICATIONS: Social Media How-To's, Creating Communities, 8 hours, 06/22/10; CPR, 4 hours, 9/2009; and First Aid, 4 hours, 9/2009.

PROFESSIONAL PUBLICATIONS: Student Ambassadors: Connecting Campuses to Energy; posted to the DOE Blog September 2010. The Intern Experience; a quarterly newsletter for DOE Interns. Life Before Last (Biographical Information).

COMPUTER SKILLS: Able to quickly learn computer software. Proficient in Microsoft Word, Excel, PowerPoint, Outlook; QuickBooks Pro and Internet and web 2.0 applications, including Facebook, Second Life, MySpace, LinkedIn, Flickr, Twitter.

LANGUAGE SKILLS: Knowledge of Spanish (oral and written).

HONORS/AFFILIATIONS: Member, National Society of Collegiate Scholars. Student member, Beyond the Classroom.

RACHEL BELL -- HIRED!
Student Trainee, New Media Specialist (HR),
GS-1099-7/9
   BA, English and Linguistics (double major)

Traditional Paper Format: 2-Page Private Industry Resume

RACHEL BELL
1234 Doorpost Rd. • College Park, MD 20741
Cell: 443-333-3333 • Email: rachelbell@email.com

PROFILE: Dynamic, self-driven, and collaborative Human Resources Management student graduating with a Master of Science degree in May 20xx. Strong interpersonal, customer relations, organizational, and oral and written communication skills. Experience providing administrative support for projects and programs. Goal-oriented, high-energy individual with excellent attention to detail. Proven analytical and research skills; ability to identify significant factors, gather pertinent data, and recognize solutions. Personable, professional, and responsible; cooperative and courteous to co-workers and customers.

EDUCATION

Enrolled in Master of Science (MS) program, Human Resource Management, Strayer University; Washington, DC; completed 9 credits; anticipated graduation date 05/20xx; GPA: 3.5
Papers / Projects:
 • Wrote major paper on human resources theory and management practices, exploring strategic role of management of core functions: total rewards, talent management, organizational development, HR information systems, and employee and labor relations.
 • Led five-person team on research project on leadership and organizational behavior. Project analyzed interaction of individual, group, and organizational dynamics that influence human behavior in organizations. Based on findings, determined appropriate management approaches to foster productive work environment.
 • Delivered HR information systems presentation at a nationwide conference. Analyzed information technologies and systems used to maintain HR data of a hypothetical organization.

Bachelor of Arts, English and Linguistics (double major); University of Maryland; College Park, MD; 05/2010; GPA: 3.67; Study abroad: University of Sheffield, Sheffield, England, 09/2008-06/2009
 • *Relevant Coursework:* Digital Writing; Social Media Strategies; Marketing & Social Media; Managing the Digital Enterprise
 • *Key Projects:* Created a "university life" blog that gained on- and off- campus audiences.

Diploma, Century High School, Eldersburg, MD, 2006

WORK EXPERIENCE

Outline Format with keywords underlined

New Media Specialist (HR), GS-1099-07, Student Trainee   05/2011–Present
U.S. Department of Energy   Washington, DC

 • <u>Project Coordination:</u> In developmental capacity, perform assignments and training in social media activities and strategies. Projects involve blogging, community development and management, social bookmarking, and commenting. Select appropriate social media tools and outlets. Support goal of recruiting top talent and branding the DOE as an "Employer of Choice."
 • <u>Social Media Initiatives:</u> Assist with creation of social media strategy to increase visibility, membership, and traffic across DOE employment brand. Monitor trends in social media tools and applications. Develop DOEJobs Twitter account to promote DOE jobs and job fairs.

- <u>Teamwork and Communication:</u> Design and execute strategies to engage both internal and external DOE stakeholders. Coordinate efforts with the CIO and Office of Public Affairs. Gather and present information on marketing and branding initiative to 18 offices. Develop factual information, draft, and publish content for social media use; review for accuracy and compliance with organizational policy.

➢ *Key Accomplishment:* Initiated roll-out of DOE/HC's social media presence by coordinating contributors across 18 HR offices. Created and delivered presentations on using social media for recruitment; designed and developed a high-visibility, high-traffic blog. RESULTS: Substantially increased DOE's social media presence; gained 5,000+ followers on LinkedIn.

Employment Solutions Division Intern
U.S. Department of Energy

01/2010–05/2011
Washington, DC

On six-person Employment Solutions Division team, supported recruitment and retention initiatives for Office of Chief Human Capital Officer, with focus on social media and marketing efforts.

- <u>Program Support:</u> Supported DOE recruiting programs, including intern, veteran and social media outreach. Collaborated on recruitment for 16 field offices and labs, organizing local recruitment events. Attended eight recruitment events to highlight DOE as "Employer of Choice." Scheduled meetings and provided administrative and programmatic support to leadership. Tracked inventory of recruiting and marketing materials for 18 offices.
- <u>Reports / Administration:</u> Collaborated on intern hire report, tracking DOE intern demographics for five years. Compiled and entered data on race, gender, schools, job series retention, creating Excel spreadsheets and charts to measure effectiveness of HR recruitment and retention initiatives. Final report identified hiring trends and quantified return on investment at recruiting events. Developed procedures for online recruitment efforts for social media. Researched potential college and university partners for social media and virtual efforts. Prepared partnership letters and monthly summer intern newsletters.

➢ *Key Project:* Edited 110-page DOE "Federal Intern Guide" for employees.

Facility Supervisor
Emerson Recreation Center, University of Maryland

08/2007–07/2010
College Park, MD

- <u>Customer Service/Supervision:</u> Answered questions, provided information, and resolved customer issues. Supervised four-person staff; assigned tasks and ensured staff adhered to customer service standards.
- <u>Facility Management:</u> Oversaw building operations, including maintenance, safety, and security. Checked regularly for spills, safety hazards, and proper equipment functioning.

EXTRACURRICULAR / VOLUNTEER ACTIVITIES

Beyond the Classroom, 09/2009–05/2010: Participated in yearlong Living and Learning Program exploring civic and social issues to develop leadership skills and civic engagement.
Maryland Images, 03/2007–05/2009: Gave tours to prospective University of Maryland College Park students and their families, providing information and tactfully answering difficult questions.

TRAINING / CERTIFICATIONS: Social Media How-To's, Creating Communities, 8 hours, 06/22/2010; CPR, 4 hours, 09/11/2009; First Aid, 4 hours, 09/10/2009

COMPUTER SKILLS: Microsoft Word, Excel, PowerPoint, Outlook; QuickBooks Pro; Internet; Facebook, Second Life, MySpace, LinkedIn, Flickr, Twitter, YouTube, Tumblr

HONORS/AFFILIATIONS: Member, National Society of Collegiate Scholars

EMMANUEL WILLIS -- HIRED!
Contract Specialist, GS-9/12
Defense Contract Management Agency

BS, International Business/Spanish Minor

Masters of Business Administration (MBA)

USAJOBS Upload Format

Emmanuel Willis

32123 Clark Drive • Tulsa, Oklahoma 74171

Phone 918-333-3333 • Dorm Phone 918-555-5555 • E-mail

emmanuel.j.willis@oru.edu

OBJECTIVE To obtain an entry level position as a business partner that will strengthen my skills while developing new ones.

Technical skills are critical to stand out

TECHNICAL SKILLS Proficient in Microsoft Word, Excel, Java, C++, Cisco, Networking 1, and PowerPoint. Demonstrated website development and management experience. Working knowledge of Electronic Data Work flow (EDW), Mechanization of Contract Administrative Services (MOCAS), Modification Delivery Order (MDO), and Wide Area Work Flow (WAWF). Skilled operating copier, multi-line phone system, and scanner. Knowledge of preparing and maintaining sensitive personnel records. Type 65 words per minute.

EDUCATION **Texas A&M University**
Masters of Business Administration (M.B.A.); Texas A&M University; Commerce, Texas; May 2012; current GPA: 3.5.

Oral Roberts University, Tulsa, Oklahoma
2009- Bachelor of Science in International Business/Spanish Minor
2007- Associates Degree - Oral Roberts University
2005- International Business Major
- Prepares students for international firms
- Focuses on management concentration

Papers and projects are described in detail

SENIOR PAPER TEAM PROJECT: Consisted of three team members taking a local owned business and preparing a 75-page research paper. Proposed utilizing different financial, marketing, and management strategies to generate more income and improve overall quality of the business. Each member of the team took a section of the project which consisted of 25 pages of research, i.e., surveys, Strength, Weakness, Opportunities, and Threat analysis (SWOT), confidential company financials, financial ratios, new proposed marketing plan, and supply chain analysis. 82% of findings implemented. Reduced debt ratio for the business by ten percent.

STRATEGIC MANAGEMENT TEAM PROJECT: Researched major Fortune 500 national grocery chain and prepared a 130-page analysis of the overall status of the company. Analyzed complex industry to determine where company could become more effective and profitable. Utilized more than 30 hours of research on key information such as general economic conditions, top competitors, supply chain, value chain analysis, competitive strength assessments, and internal analysis. Submitted new business ideas, strategies, and proposed business plan to the grocery chain for acquisition, negotiation of contracts for property rentals, and expansion mergers locally and nationally. Designed, edited, and presented 75 minute PowerPoint presentation on project results. Team received an above average grade on the project.

INTERNATIONAL BUSINESS PROJECT: Compared economies in emerging markets of Brazil, Russia, India, and China. Researched similarities and differences such as Gross Domestic Product, purchasing power parity, exchange rates, real growth rate and local trading agreements or organizations, and contract negotiations among the four. Organized, planned and presented 75-minute presentation with question and answer period to peers and raters. A current UN delegate to Afghanistan was present and attempted to recruit for employment opportunities after presentation.

FINANCIAL MANAGEMENT PROJECT: Independent project which was required to be completed under strict time constraints. Compared the overall financial status of Dell and Apple. Analyzed profit margin, debt ratios, stocks, bonds, annuities, inventory ratio and net income, and net loss. Researched all financials for each company to determine competitive advantage in the computer industry. Provided rating professor with investment options and net return forecast of both Dell and Apple.

OTHER MAJOR COURSE PROJECTS INCLUDED:
- Marketing strategy for innovative design of SUV International Marketing for utilizing cultural awareness of new product.
- Quantitative Analysis to enhance value of chain performance.
- Statistics: conducted and administered customer contract surveys.
- Graduate Management economic and comparative analysis of countries.
- Graduate Finance practical analysis of bank foreclosure, revamping, and institutionalizing new entities.

TEAM PROJECT LEADERSHIP SKILLS: Served as team leader on 12+ significant projects, which developed skill in analyzing projects, delegating tasks, and establishing and implementing and adhering to timelines. Developed the following business and project management skills:

- Draft project details, to include resolving team conflicts, organizing team meetings, supervising tasks
- Develop innovative marketing concepts and strategies
- Create alternative methods of standard analysis for problem solving

- SWOT Analysis to reduce company debt by 10%
- Assist in contract negotiations
- Implement business strategies to improve quality of business
- Evaluate foreign debt, policy, and economic improvements
- Create positive work environment for the team

COMMUNITY ACHIEVEMENTS:
- Mission Trips to Poland and Madagascar (April 2005). Assisted in operation of English cafes. Presented to numerous churches, universities, and local businessmen motivational and inspirational workshops and seminars.
- Mission Trip to Ireland (May 2005). Opened dialogue with youth in churches. Designed, planned and facilitated seminars on relationship building. Authored an instruction manual to further enhance learning.
- U.S. Governor Campaign, Washington D.C. (November 2005). Distributed literature, encouraged registered voters to participate, and promoted candidate's position on political issues.

WORK EXPERIENCE

Child Development Center, Geilenkirchen, Germany
Educational Program Technician, June 2008-August 2008

Supervised activities in a variety of rooms that served children ranging in age from 14 months to 12 years old. Provided warm, supportive environment for developing emotional and social growth. Provided instruction in three languages: English, Spanish, and German. Individualized instruction, enhanced communication and improved cultural awareness within the group. As one of 15 member staff, assisted in planning daily agenda to advance social and motor development activities including art, cooking, storytelling, music, supervised play, and field trips.

Active participant in staff meetings, initiated communication with parents to resolve concerns and behavioral deficiencies. Strong participant in team efforts and cooperative behavior. Encouraged parental input into all phases to generate a new cooperative atmosphere for the children, staff, and community.

ACER Networking America, Tulsa, Oklahoma
Technician/Customer Service Specialist, Sept 2007-Feb 2008
Helped network and troubleshoot all Acer desktops and laptops. Provided great customer care and service for Acer customers. Upheld all company regulations and Code of Business Conduct by enforcing loss prevention policies and communicating violations to the supervisory team. Assisted management team in establishing goals and priorities of staff.

Reported customer feedback and provided input in direct services to maximize productivity standards to upper management. Individualized marketing and sales strategy resulting in record local net profit. A strong participant in team selling. Handled competitive situation with competence and tact. Skilled in refusing customer requests while presenting alternative solutions. Modeled and encouraged a healthy work environment amongst staff brand associates, achieving first rate team dynamics.

Joint Forces Command Brunssum, Netherlands
Data Processing Specialist, June 2005-July 2005
Processed confidential records and complied with Privacy Act of 1974. Developed, maintained, and updated all filing systems. Assisted with data entry. Saved important historical data history for clients by effectively troubleshooting files. Tested new data programs for bugs on the installation and documented them for programmers to correct. Analyzed the capabilities and features of all new electronic equipment and products before distribution to the work units and squadrons.

SIGNIFICANT ACCOMPLISHMENTS: A main speaker for International Business Conference of Montego Bay, Jamaica. One of 5 students selected to present to 200 multi-disciplined business leaders attending conference from 12 different nations. Gave ten minute presentation in Spanish, which increased awareness of cultural diversity in business to conference attendees. Utilized innovative fundraising ideas and was self-motivated to raise over $2,500 to attend conference. Designed an instructor's manual for all who attended on how to achieve and maintain a competitive advantage in the business arena.

Yokota 374ᵗʰ Airbase, Tokyo, Japan
Maintenance Squadron , June 2004- July 2004 and June 2003 – August 2003
Processed records for temporary applicants seeking employment. Performed office duties such as filing, typing, running errands and updating system files. Designed PowerPoint presentations.

VOLUNTEER
EXPERIENCE

- Mission trip to Montego Bay, Jamaica May 15, 2007-May 27, 2007; One of the main speakers for the International Business Conference of Montego Bay (IBCMB)

- Mission trip to Madagascar, May 2006-June 2006; helped run English cafes, talked to various churches and universities in the capital and coast, donated many items to orphanages, gave many motivational and success speeches to pastors and local residents.

- Worked for Republican National Committee, November 2005; helped run campaign for Governor Kilgore in Washington, D.C.

- Mission trip to Ireland, May 2005; spoke to many youth in churches, presented relationship building seminars.

- Mission trip to Poland, April 2005; built playgrounds and helped in English cafes.

- Musician for praise and worship team May 2003-July 2004.

- Drummer for Youth & Adult choir June 2002-July 2004.

AWARDS RECEIVED

Presidents Volunteer Service Award 2007, Presidents Volunteer Service Award 2006 Washington D.C., Model NATO 2005 Award, Athletic Academic All-Conference Award 2004-2005, Leading Offensive Scorer 2004-2005 basketball season, Captain of basketball team 2004-2005, Lettered in 3 varsity sports in one academic year 2003-2004, 3 years honor roll, Captain of Junior Varsity Football and basketball team 2001-2002.

SKILLS

Java, Website Development and Management, C++, 65 wpm, Microsoft Word, PowerPoint, Excel, Cisco Networking 1, diverse in cultural populations.

LANGUAGES

Advanced Spanish, Beginner Japanese, currently studying German

INTERESTS & ACTIVITIES

Track and Field, Band, Church Youth Group, Teen & Adult Choir musician, Junior Varsity Football, Varsity Football, Junior Varsity Basketball, Varsity Basketball, Playing percussion instruments, Computer Science, Model European Parliament, The Hague International Model United Nations, NATO, Interacting with different cultures, Future Business Leaders of America 2004-2005 (F.B.L.A.) African American Student Union 2005-2006 (A.A.S.U.).

REFERENCES

NAME: WILLIE SHORT
LOCATION: U.S. ARMY GARRISON SCHINNEN, NETHERLANDS
POSITION: COMMUNITY RECREATION CHIEF
PHONE NUMBER: 00031464437488
E-MAIL: WILLIE.SHORT@EUR.ARMY.MIL
REFERENCE TYPE: PROFESSIONAL

EMMANUEL WILLIS -- HIRED!
Contract Specialist, GS-9/12
Defense Contract Management Agency
BS, International Business/Spanish Minor
Masters of Business Administration (MBA)

Traditional Paper Format: 2-Page Private Industry Resume

Emmanuel Willis

32123 Clark Drive • Tulsa, Oklahoma 74171
Phone 918-333-3333 • Phone 918-555-5555 • E-mail
emmanuel.j.willis@oru.edu

OBJECTIVE
To obtain an entry level position as a business partner that will strengthen my skills while developing new ones.

TECHNICAL SKILLS
Proficient in Microsoft Word, Excel, Java, C++, Cisco, Networking 1, and PowerPoint. Demonstrated website development and management experience. Advanced Spanish, Beginner Japanese, currently studying German.
Public Speaking and Presentation Building … Team Leader … Business Analyst … Researcher … Data Manager … Supply Chain Knowledge

EDUCATION

Texas A&M University
Masters of Business Administration (M.B.A.); Texas A&M University; Commerce, Texas; expected May 2014; current GPA: 3.5.

Oral Roberts University, Tulsa, Oklahoma
Bachelor of Science in International Business/Spanish Minor, 2012

SENIOR PAPER TEAM PROJECT: Consisted of three team members taking a local owned business and preparing a 75-page research paper. Proposed utilizing different financial, marketing, and management strategies to generate more income and improve overall quality of the business. Resulted in implementation of 82% of the findings. Reduced debt ratio for the business by ten percent.

STRATEGIC MANAGEMENT TEAM PROJECT: Researched major Fortune 500 national grocery chain and prepared a 130-page analysis of the overall status of the company. Analyzed complex industry to determine where company could become more effective and profitable. Utilized more than 30 hours of research on key information such as general economic conditions, top competitors, supply chain, value chain analysis, competitive strength assessments, and internal analysis.

INTERNATIONAL BUSINESS PROJECT: Compared economies in emerging markets of Brazil, Russia, India, and China. Researched similarities and differences such as Gross Domestic Product, purchasing power parity, exchange rates, real growth rate and local trading agreements or organizations, and contract negotiations among the four.

FINANCIAL MANAGEMENT PROJECT: Compared the overall financial status of Dell and Apple. Analyzed profit margin, debt ratios, stocks, bonds, annuities, inventory ratio and net income, and net loss.

OTHER MAJOR COURSE PROJECTS INCLUDED:
- Marketing strategy for innovative design of SUV International Marketing for

utilizing cultural awareness of new product.
- Quantitative Analysis to enhance value of chain performance.
- Statistics: conducted and administered customer contract surveys.
- Graduate Management economic and comparative analysis of countries.
- Graduate Finance practical analysis of bank foreclosure, revamping, and institutionalizing new entities.

TEAM PROJECT LEADERSHIP SKILLS: Served as team leader on 12+ significant projects, which developed skill in analyzing projects, delegating tasks, and establishing and implementing and adhering to timelines.

WORK EXPERIENCE

Child Development Center, Geilenkirchen, Germany
Educational Program Technician, June 2013-August 2013
Provided instruction in three languages: English, Spanish, and German for children ages 14 months to 12 years. As one of 15 member staff, planned daily activities.

ACER Networking America, Tulsa, Oklahoma
Technician/Customer Service Specialist, Sept 2012-Feb 2012
Helped network and troubleshoot all Acer desktops and laptops. Upheld all company regulations and Code of Business Conduct by enforcing loss prevention policies and communicating violations to the supervisory team. Assisted management team in establishing goals and priorities of staff.

Joint Forces Command Brunssum, Netherlands
Data Processing Specialist, June 2011-July 2011
Processed confidential records and complied with Privacy Act of 1974. Saved important historical data history for clients by effectively troubleshooting files. Tested new data programs for bugs on the installation and documented them for programmers to correct. Analyzed the capabilities and features of all new electronic equipment and products before distribution to the work units and squadrons.

Recruited as an invited speaker for International Business Conference of Montego Bay, Jamaica. One of 5 students selected to present to 200 multi-disciplined business leaders attending conference from 12 different nations.

Yokota 374th Airbase, Tokyo, Japan
Maintenance Squadron, June 2010 – Aug. 2010
Processed records for temporary applicants seeking employment. Performed office duties such as filing, typing, running errands and updating system files. Designed PowerPoint presentations.

VOLUNTEER EXPERIENCE

- Mission trips to Montego Bay, Jamaica; Madagascar, Ireland and Poland as musician, speaker, playground builder and mentor. (2010-2011)

AWARDS RECEIVED

Presidents Volunteer Service Award 2009, Presidents Volunteer Service Award 2010 Washington D.C., Model NATO 2009 Award, Athletic Academic All-Conference Award 2008, Leading Offensive Scorer, 2008 basketball season, Captain of basketball team 2010, Lettered in 3 varsity sports in one academic year 2010, 3 years honor roll, Captain of Junior Varsity football and basketball team 2009 -2010

SCOTT HAMPSTEAD -- HIRED!
Mechanical Engineer, GS-9/12
US Army Corps of Engineers
    BS, Mechanical Engineering Honors Program

USAJOBS Resume Builder Format

SCOTT HAMPSTEAD
5555 University Boulevard
Hyattsville, MD 20783
Phone: (301) 333-3333
Email: scottmhampstead@hotmail.com

[JOB BLOCK 1]
B.S. IN MECHANICAL ENGINEERING HONORS PROGRAM
University of Maryland, College Park, MD
Expected July 2012   Overall GPA: 3.6/4.0   Engineering GPA: 3.7/4.0

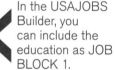

In the USAJOBS Builder, you can include the education as JOB BLOCK 1.

HONORS AND ACTIVITIES
National Merit Scholar, Maryland Distinguished Scholar
A.P. Scholar with Honors, Dean's List (4 times)
Maryland Club Lacrosse (2006-2009); Maryland Intramural Soccer (2008)

RELATED COURSEWORK
Calculus, physics, chemistry, differential equations, statistics, dynamics, thermodynamics, introduction to MATlab, fluid mechanics, electronics and instrumentation, engineering materials and manufacturing processes, statistical methods of product development, transfer processes, vibrations controls and optimization, product engineering and manufacturing, automotive design, manufacturing automation, technical writing, human resource management, introduction to transportation in supply chain management.

COMPUTER SKILLS: Word, Excel, PowerPoint, Pro-Engineer, MATlab.

JOB BLOCK 2 is a listing of college projects and a description of each project.

[JOB BLOCK 2]
University of Maryland College Park, 2005 to present

Team Semester Projects:
REDESIGN OF THE DEWALT TRADESMAN DRILL using the nine-step product development process. Directed the testing and building of a prototype cordless/corded drill. Compared results to necessary specifications to determine effectiveness of the design. Gave PowerPoint presentations on project results. Utilized analytical tools such as the House of Quality, Weighted Decision Matrix, Morphological Chart, and Functional Decomposition to redesign drill. 2009

DESIGN OF HYBRID SUV FOR FUTURETRUCK COMPETITION. In charge of testing of the performance of the electric motor. Analyzed complex schematics to determine connector specifications and location. Negotiated the donation of connectors for the high-voltage system. Researched torque curves for the stock engine and the replacement engine. 2007-2008

DESIGN OF MATLAB CODE TO MODEL AIRBORNE CONCENTRATIONS OF DUST IN TURBULENT WINDS. Modeled winds with force vectors. Displayed results in multiple plots corresponding to different wind conditions. Experimented swith different mesh densities to determine the degree of computing power necessary for accurate results. 2007

OTHER PROJECTS HAVE INCLUDED:
Design of portable water pump
Statistical analysis of campus traffic flow
Evaluation of scale wind tunnel testing of a high-rise building
Analysis of stress, bending and failure in a lug wrench

[JOB BLOCK 3]
University of Maryland, College Park, MD; Team Project Skills

 JOB BLOCK 3 is a summary of team lead skills for each project.

AS TEAM LEADER for more than 10 significant projects, developed skill in analyzing projects, delegating tasks and establishing timelines. Also developed the following engineering and project management skills:
-Draft project details
-Devise and recommend alternative methods of standardized analysis as a basis for solving problems
-Recommend and devise deviations to details
-Assist in reviews of engineering changes
-Review compliance to contract during design, development and production
-Evaluate control of baseline products
-Manage and/or witness tests
-Evaluate quality assurance activities
-Conduct cost and schedule analysis and estimations
-Manage engineering data collection and analysis

[JOB BLOCK 4]
Sales Clerk, Village Antiques, 2787 Oella Ave., Oella, MD 21228; 2005-2009; Supervisor: John Jones, 410-333-3333; salary: $10 per hour; Responsible for customer service, sales, daily operation of store (25 hours per week).

Education is repeated in the EDUCATION section in the USAJOBS Builder.

EDUCATION:

B.S. IN MECHANICAL ENGINEERING HONORS PROGRAM, 2009
University of Maryland, College Park, MD
Diploma, Centennial High School, Ellicott City, MD, Class of 2005

AWARDS AND RECOGNITIONS:
College:
Overall GPA: 3.65/4.0, Engineering GPA: 3.75/4.0

High School Academic Honors:
Honor Roll; Cumulative GPA: 3.6 / 4.0; National Merit Finalist/Scholar; A.P. Scholar with Honors

High School Significant Courses:
Gifted and Talented English, Social Studies; Math and Science course work
A.P. Psychology, A.P. Statistics; A.P. English 12, A.P. U.S. History; A.P. Calculus I and II

OTHER INFORMATION:
Active in basketball, racquetball and lacrosse throughout high school and college. Attended University of Hawaii, Oahu, Summer 2007 studying Hawaiian culture, surfing and golf. Traveled to France and Denmark, Summer 2005.

SCOTT HAMPSTEAD -- HIRED!
Mechanical Engineer, GS-9/12
US Army Corps of Engineers
BS, Mechanical Engineering Honors Program

Traditional Paper Format: 2-Page Private Industry Resume

SCOTT HAMPSTEAD
5555 University Boulevard
Hyattsville, MD 20783
Phone: (301) 333-3333
Email: scottmhampstead@hotmail.com

OBJECTIVE:

MECHANICAL ENGINEER; TEAM LEAD; PROJECT MANAGER; TEST MANAGER

SUMMARY OF QUALIFICATIONS:

AS TEAM LEADER for more than 10 significant engineering projects, developed skill in analyzing projects, delegating tasks and establishing timelines. Also developed the following engineering and project management skills:
-Draft project details
-Devise and recommend alternative methods of standardized analysis as a basis for solving problems
-Recommend and devise deviations to details
-Assist in reviews of engineering changes
-Review compliance to contract during design, development and production
-Evaluate control of baseline products
-Manage and/or witness tests
-Evaluate quality assurance activities
-Conduct cost and schedule analysis and estimations
-Manage engineering data collection and analysis

COMPUTER SKILLS: Word, Excel, PowerPoint, Pro-Engineer, MATlab.

EDUCATION:

B.S. IN MECHANICAL ENGINEERING HONORS PROGRAM
University of Maryland, College Park, MD
Expected July 2014
Overall GPA: 3.6/4.0   Engineering GPA: 3.7/4.0

RELATED COURSEWORK
- Calculus, physics, chemistry, differential equations, statistics, dynamics, thermodynamics, intro to MATlab, fluid mechanics, electronics and instrumentation, engineering materials and manufacturing processes, statistical methods of product development, transfer processes, vibrations controls and optimization, product

engineering and manufacturing, automotive design, manufacturing automation, technical writing, intro to transportation in supply chain management.

Team Semester Projects:

- **REDESIGN OF THE DEWALT TRADESMAN DRILL** using the nine-step product development process. Directed the testing and building of a prototype cordless/corded drill. Compared results to necessary specifications to determine effectiveness of the design. Gave PowerPoint presentations on project results. Utilized analytical tools such as the House of Quality, Weighted Decision Matrix, Morphological Chart, and Functional Decomposition to redesign drill. 2013

- **DESIGN OF HYBRID SUV FOR FUTURETRUCK COMPETITION.** In charge of testing the performance of the electric motor. Analyzed complex schematics to determine connector specifications and location. Negotiated the donation of connectors for the high-voltage system. Researched torque curves for the stock engine and the replacement engine. 2011-2012

- **DESIGN OF MATLAB CODE TO MODEL AIRBORNE CONCENTRATIONS OF DUST IN TURBULENT WINDS**. Modeled winds with force vectors. Displayed results in multiple plots corresponding to different wind conditions. Experimented with different mesh densities to determine the degree of computing power necessary for accurate results. 2010

OTHER PROJECTS HAVE INCLUDED:
- Design of portable water pump
- Statistical analysis of campus traffic flow
- Evaluation of scale wind tunnel testing of a high-rise building
- Analysis of stress, bending and failure in a lug wrench

HONORS AND ACTIVITIES
National Merit Scholar, Maryland Distinguished Scholar
A.P. Scholar with Honors, Dean's List (4 times)
Maryland Club Lacrosse (2006-2009); Maryland Intramural Soccer (2008)

OTHER EXPERIENCE:
Sales Clerk, Village Antiques, 2787 Oella Ave., Oella, MD 21228; 2009-present; Supervisor: John Jones, 410-333-3333; Family Business. Responsible for customer service, sales, daily operation of store (25 hours per week).

OTHER INFORMATION:
Active in basketball, racquetball and lacrosse throughout college. Attended University of Hawaii, Oahu, Summer 2009. Traveled to France and Denmark, Summer 2008.

JEREMY DENTON -- HIRED!
INTELLIGENCE ANALYST, GS-9/12
Department of Homeland Security
US Marine Corps, E-5

BA, Government and Public Policy

USAJOBS Upload Format

JEREMY D. DENTON

1234 Anywhere Street
City, State, Zipcode
Phone: 555.555.5555
Email: jeremy.d.denton@gmail.com

OBJECTIVE: Career Ladder Position, Pathways Program, Management Analyst, Intelligence Analyst, Security Specialist

PROFESSIONAL EXPERIENCE:

- Substantial leadership and planning experience as Helicopter Crew Chief in USMC.
- Skilled in critical thinking, analysis and data management.
- Outstanding record of achievement as Pilot with 16 Air Medals.
- US Marine Corps, 08/2003 to 01/2008, honorable discharge
- Security Clearance: Secret (active), Interim Top Secret (active)

EDUCATION:

Bachelor of Arts, Government and Public Policy, *cum laude*. University of Baltimore, Maryland. GPA: 3.7 out of 4.0; January 2010.

- DRAFTED MAJOR PAPER ON LEGAL NORMS: Successfully drafted and submitted a paper exploring the organization, function and processes of law making institutions in the American justice system. The paper also analyzed legal ethics and their role in major cases over a five-year period.

- LED TEAM PROJECT ON GOVERNANCE: Coordinated research and writing efforts of 2 other students on a major governance project. Reviewed fundamental theories of governance, researched literature on related topics, and drafted a recommendation-focused paper on "best practices" in public administration.
- CO-PRESENTED PAPER AT MAJOR CONFERENCE: Participated in a panel presentation at the national Conference on Ethics and Social Justice. Delivered prepared commentary on ethical challenges in government leadership, through the lenses of disparity, power and privilege.

International Marine Transportation, New York Maritime College, Bronx, NY, 35 credits, 09/2002-05/2003.

PROFESSIONAL EXPERIENCE

01/2010 to present, **INTELLIGENCE ANALYST**; E-5; Maryland National Guard (Reserves), Baltimore, MD,

- DATABASE ADMINISTRATOR: Maintain, process, and manage security clearance database and associated procedures for 1-175th Infantry Battalion utilizing JPA. Initiate clearance process for personnel requiring new clearances, and identify personnel whose authorization has been revoked. Process and secure sensitive and/or derogatory personnel information in close coordination with Army security managers. Enter coded information into Army systems.

- TRAINING: Lead numerous classes on Army critical skills and required knowledge, including Operational Security and Human Trafficking.

- SAFEGUARDING PERSONAL INFORMATION: Protect file integrity of 600+ individual files, each containing sensitive personal information.

- OPERATION PLANNING: Help plan real world training exercises for upcoming peacekeeping deployment to the Sinai Peninsula in support of 1979 Camp David Accords.

KEY ACCOMPLISHMENTS:
- SELECTED TO BE BATALLION ELECTRONIC WARFARE NON-COMMISSIONED OFFICER: Outstanding work ethic led to selection as the Battalion Electronic Warfare NCO. As EWO, trained to use the electromagnetic spectrum to deny the enemy's ability to attack US and Allied personnel with remote devices. Work directly with commanders to ensure the proper utilization of Electronic Warfare to safeguard friendly personnel.

10/2004-01/2008, **HELICOPTER CREW CHIEF**; E-5, Sgt, 3rd Marine Air Wing, Marine Corps Air Station Miramar, San Diego, CA

- TEAM LEAD / FLIGHT CREW MEMBER: Planned, organized, led, and performed maintenance on CH-53E Super Stallion helicopters, including during Operation Iraqi Freedom. Supported more than 2,000 sorties in several major campaigns.

- SCHEDULING AND COORDINATION: Performed daily inspections on assigned aircraft; assisted in preflight inspections performing final checks; monitored aircraft performance during flight; assisted as a lookout and advised pilot of obstacles and other aircraft.

- CRITICAL THINKING AND PROBLEM SOLVING: Analyzed weight, mission, cargo and prepared aircraft for maximum defense. Utilized evaluative and technical skills in operating aircraft mounted weapons systems.

- PLAN AND ORGANIZE WORK: Assisted in the supervision and administration of aircraft maintenance operations. Developed methods and procedures to improve efficiency of the Flight Crew, especially in flight operations or emergency maintenance procedures.

KEY ACCOMPLISHMENTS:
- LOGGED 1,200+ FLIGHT HOURS WITHOUT A SINGLE LOSS OF LIFE OR AIRCRAFT during two tours in Iraq and in the United States, including during combat conditions, armed interdictions, border patrolling, and medical evacuations of military and civilians.

- AS CAPTAIN, performed essential systems and safety checks for every aircraft under my care daily prior to operations (up to 14 helicopters). Led team effort in achieving a perfect safety record for my unit over 3.5 years and two combat tours.

MILITARY TRAINING

Naval Aviation Air Crewman Candidate School at NATTC, NAS Pensacola, FL.
Survival, Evasion, Resistance, and Escape (SERE) School at Brunswick, ME.
"A" and "C" school, CH-53E Crew Chief Training Syllabus
Plane Captain (PC) Ground syllabus for type aircraft.

AWARDS AND RECOGNITION

Navy/USMC Achievement Medal, 2007
2 Iraq Campaign Medals, 2007, 2004
16 Air Medals
USMC Good Conduct Medal, 2006
Global War on Terrorism Service Medal, 2004
National Defense Service Medal, 2003
Sea Service Deployment Ribbon
Expert Rifle Badge and Expert Pistol Badge (2d Award)

OTHER INFORMATION:

Maryland Drivers License; Current Interim Top Secret Government clearance
Eagle Scout, Boy Scouts of America; CPR and First Aid Certified through the Red Cross

JEREMY DENTON -- HIRED!
INTELLIGENCE ANALYST, GS-9/12
Department of Homeland Security
US Marine Corps, E-5
BA, Government and Public Policy

Traditional Paper Format: 2-Page Private Industry Resume

JEREMY D. DENTON
1234 Anywhere Street
City, State, Zipcode
Phone: 555.555.5555
Email: jeremy.d.denton@gmail.com

OBJECTIVE: Management Analyst, Intelligence Analyst, Security Specialist

PROFESSIONAL EXPERIENCE:

- Substantial leadership and planning experience as Helicopter Crew Chief in USMC.
- Skilled in critical thinking, analysis and data management.
- Outstanding record of achievement as Pilot with 16 Air Medals.
- US Marine Corps, 08/2003 to 01/2008, honorable discharge
- Security Clearance: Secret (active), Interim Top Secret (active)

EDUCATION:

Bachelor of Arts, Government and Public Policy, *cum laude.* University of Baltimore, Maryland. GPA: 3.7 out of 4.0; January 2010. *(Thanks to the GI Bill!)*

International Marine Transportation, New York Maritime College, Bronx, NY, 35 credits, 09/2002-05/2003.

PROFESSIONAL EXPERIENCE

OUTLINE FORMAT also works for a private industry resume.

01/2010 to present, **INTELLIGENCE ANALYST**; E-5; Maryland National Guard (Reserves), Baltimore, MD,

- DATABASE ADMINISTRATOR: Maintain, process, and manage security clearance database and associated procedures for 1-175th Infantry Battalion utilizing JPA. Protect file integrity of 600+ individual files, each containing sensitive personal information.
- TRAINING: Lead numerous classes on Army critical skills and required knowledge, including Operational Security and Human Trafficking.

KEY ACCOMPLISHMENTS:
- Help plan real world training exercises for upcoming peacekeeping deployment to the Sinai Peninsula in support of 1979 Camp David Accords.
- Outstanding work ethic led to selection as the Battalion Electronic Warfare NCO.

10/2004-01/2008, **HELICOPTER CREW CHIEF**; E-5, Sgt, 3rd Marine Air Wing, Marine Corps Air Station Miramar, San Diego, CA

- TEAM LEAD / FLIGHT CREW MEMBER: Planned, organized, led, and performed maintenance on CH-53E Super Stallion helicopters, including during Operation Iraqi Freedom. Supported more than 2,000 sorties in several major campaigns.

- SCHEDULING AND COORDINATION: Performed daily inspections on assigned aircraft; assisted in preflight inspections performing final checks; monitored aircraft performance during flight; assisted as a lookout and advised pilot of obstacles and other aircraft.

- CRITICAL THINKING AND PROBLEM SOLVING: Analyzed weight, mission, cargo and prepared aircraft for maximum defense. Utilized evaluative and technical skills in operating aircraft mounted weapons systems.

- PLAN AND ORGANIZE WORK: Assisted in the supervision and administration of aircraft maintenance operations. Developed methods and procedures to improve efficiency of the Flight Crew, especially in flight operations or emergency maintenance procedures.

- TRAINING / COMMUNICATIONS: Using effective verbal and written communication skills, trained junior Marines in every aspect of the Marine Corps, including history, financial education, alcohol awareness, and professional development. Trained junior staff in aircraft operations, aerial gunnery, combat tactics.

KEY ACCOMPLISHMENTS:
- LOGGED 1,200+ FLIGHT HOURS WITHOUT A SINGLE LOSS OF LIFE OR AIRCRAFT during two tours in Iraq and in the United States, including during combat conditions, armed interdictions, border patrolling, and medical evacuations of military and civilians.

- AS PLANE CAPTAIN, performed essential systems and safety checks for every aircraft under my care daily prior to operations (up to 14 helicopters). Led team effort in achieving a perfect safety record for my unit over 3.5 years and two combat tours.

MILITARY TRAINING
Naval Aviation Air Crewman Candidate School at NATTC, NAS Pensacola, FL.
Survival, Evasion, Resistance, and Escape (SERE) School at Brunswick, ME.
"A" and "C" school, CH-53E Crew Chief Training Syllabus.
Plane Captain (PC) Ground syllabus for type aircraft.

AWARDS AND RECOGNITION
Navy/USMC Achievement Medal, 2007
2 Iraq Campaign Medals, 2007, 2004
16 Air Medals
USMC Good Conduct Medal, 2006
Global War on Terrorism Service Medal, 2004
National Defense Service Medal, 2003
Sea Service Deployment Ribbon
Expert Rifle Badge and Expert Pistol Badge (2d Award)

OTHER INFORMATION:
Maryland Drivers License; Current Interim Top Secret Government clearance
Eagle Scout, Boy Scouts of America; CPR and First Aid Certified through the Red Cross

BRANDON BILLINGS -- HIRED!
LAW ENFORCEMENT OFFICER, GS-9/12
Department of Homeland Security
US Coast Guard, E-5
BS, Homeland Security

USAJOBS Upload Format

BRANDON B. BILLINGS
394 Aalapapa Drive, Kailua, HI 96734
Cell: (808) 222-2222

OBJECTIVE: Seeking an Internship position in Law Enforcement, offering college coursework and military experience in Homeland Security.

SPECIALIZED EXPERIENCE
THREE YEARS EXPERIENCE IN HOMELAND SECURITY:
• Harbor Patrol - Protect property and persons
• Enforce appropriate criminal codes and regulations
• Board and inspect vessels; issue citations
• Responds to crowd and riot control, and Homeland Security Threats
• Investigate crimes and interview witnesses
• Direct and assist persons to safety areas during fire, storm or other emergencies
• Evacuate persons from dangerous areas

EDUCATION

Embry-Riddle Aeronautical University, Schofield Barracks, HI
B.S. in Homeland Security, expected May 2013

Relevant Courses:
(Completed) Introduction to Homeland Security; Fundamentals of Transportation Security; Introduction to Industrial Security; Business Skills for the HS Professional; Fundamentals of Emergency Management; Critical Infrastructure and Risk Analysis; HS Law and Policy.

(To be completed by graduation) Terrorism: Origins, Ideologies & Goals; Intelligence Systems & Structures in Homeland Security; Strategic Planning & Decision Making in H.S.; Homeland Security Technology & Systems; Emerging Topics in Homeland Security; Environmental Security.

MAJOR PAPERS:

DRAFTED MAJOR DISASTER RESPONSE PAPER: Successfully completed a substantial 15-page in-depth examination of managerial strategies for resilience in disaster situations. Evaluated local community, private sector, and federal-level components in disaster response.

LED SEMESTER-LONG PROJECT: Delivered leadership and guidance for a semester long project analyzing infrastructure protection, jurisdiction, and interoperability. Presented, along with team-members, recommendations relating to protecting telecommunications and information technology networks while identifying them as vulnerable assets.

HOMELAND SECURITY CAPSTONE: Completed a capstone project evaluating vulnerabilities and protective countermeasures relating to national critical infrastructure with particular emphasis on food and water supply. Project culminated in a series of recommendations to improving the organization and management of food and water security.

Albany Community College, Albany, NY; 23 quarter hours; 2004-2005
Albany High School, Albany, NY; Diploma; 2004

WORK HISTORY

August 2009 to August 2011; U.S. Coast Guard, BOARDING TEAM MEMBER / SMALL ARMS INSTRUCTOR, Sector WaterWays Management and Security, Vessel Boarding Security Team, Honolulu, HI

- SECURITY OFFICER / CONDUCT HARBOR PATROL. Conducted harbor security patrols in emergency response vehicles of Honolulu commercial harbors, Barbers Point, Kewalo Basin, Ala Wai, and Kaneohe Bay harbors.

- HOMELAND SECURITY BOARDINGS: Monitored vessel activities within the harbor. Conducted Homeland Security boardings of all vessels entering Honolulu and Barbers Point harbors.

- DISTRESS CALLS: Assisted persons in distress and ensure security around waterways. Cooperated with emergency management and law enforcement departments.

- LAW ENFORCEMENT AND INVESTIGATION. Cooperated with and assisted federal and state law enforcement officers in detection of criminals, such as smugglers or illegal entrants. Investigated suspicious vessels and establishments in and around harbor areas. Participated in mutual law enforcement patrols with State Department of Land and Natural Resources.

- INSPECTOR. Inspected conditions of vessels and crews in compliance with and using knowledge of U.S. Coast Guard standards.

- COMMAND INTELLIGENCE OFFICER. Logged suspicious activities and sent information to senior management for review and distribution to appropriate federal and state agencies.

- FIRE ARMS INSTRUCTOR. Instructed in the handling, operation, and maintenance of small arms weapons, ammunition, and pyrotechnics, including the use of the 9 mm Beretta, M16 A1 rifle, and riot shotgun. Maintained all ordnance / gunnery equipment, including mechanical, electrical, and hydraulic.

July 2006 to Aug. 2009; DECKHAND, U.S. Coast Guard, Cutter ACUSHNET; Honolulu, HI

SAFETY AND SECURITY WATCH TEAM MEMBER. Enforced nation's laws and rescued people in trouble on waterways. Conducted search and rescue operations. Inspected ships of all sizes, from smallest watercraft to largest tankers to ensure seaworthiness and compliance with U.S. laws. Used advanced electronics, telecommunications, and computer systems.

PROFESSIONAL TRAINING

Force Protection Fundamentals, Ship Board Security Engagement Weapons
Incident Response to Terrorist Bombings Awareness, Small Arms Instructor
Damage Control Personal Qualifications Standards

PROFESSIONAL LICENSE: Captain's License – 50 ton

COMPUTER PROFICIENCIES: Microsoft Word, Excel, Access, PowerPoint

BRANDON BILLINGS -- HIRED!
LAW ENFORCEMENT OFFICER, GS-9/12
Department of Homeland Security
US Coast Guard, E-5
BS, Homeland Security

Traditional Paper Format: 2-Page Private Industry Resume

BRANDON B. BILLINGS
394 Aalapapa Drive, Kailua, HI 96734
Cell: (808) 222-3333

OBJECTIVE: POLICE OFFICER

SPECIALIZED EXPERIENCE

THREE YEARS EXPERIENCE IN LAW ENFORCEMENT:
- Harbor Patrol - Protect property and persons
- Enforce appropriate criminal codes and regulations
- Board and inspect vessels; issue citations
- Respond to crowd and riot control, and Homeland Security Threats
- Investigate crimes and Interview witnesses
- Directs and assists persons to safety areas during fire, storm or other emergencies
- Evacuate persons from dangerous areas

WORK HISTORY

August 2007 to Present; U.S. Coast Guard, BOARDING TEAM MEMBER / SMALL ARMS INSTRUCTOR, Sector WaterWays Management and Security, Vessel Boarding Security Team, Honolulu, HI

- SECURITY OFFICER / CONDUCT HARBOR PATROL. Conduct harbor security patrols in emergency response vehicles of Honolulu commercial harbors, Barbers Point, Kewalo Basin, Ala Wai, and Kaneohe Bay harbors.

- HOMELAND SECURITY BOARDINGS: Monitor vessel activities within the harbor. Conduct Homeland Security boardings of all vessels entering Honolulu and Barbers Point harbors.

- DISTRESS CALLS: Assist persons in distress and ensure security around waterways. Cooperate with emergency management and law enforcement departments.

- LAW ENFORCEMENT AND INVESTIGATION. Cooperate with and assist federal and state law enforcement officers in detection of criminals, such as smugglers or illegal entrants. Investigate suspicious vessels and establishments in and around harbor areas. Participate in mutual law enforcement patrols with State Department of Land and Natural Resources.

- INSPECTOR. Inspect conditions of vessels and crews in compliance with and using knowledge of U.S. Coast Guard standards.

- COMMAND INTELLIGENCE OFFICER. Log suspicious activities and send information to senior management for review and distribution to appropriate federal and state agencies.

- FIRE ARMS INSTRUCTOR. Instruct in the handling, operation, and maintenance of small arms weapons, ammunition, and pyrotechnics, including the use of the 9 mm Beretta, M16 A1 rifle, and riot shotgun. Maintain all ordnance / gunnery equipment, including mechanical, electrical, and hydraulic.

July 2006 to August 2007; DECKHAND, U.S. Coast Guard, Cutter ACUSHNET; Honolulu, HI

SAFETY AND SECURITY WATCH TEAM MEMBER. Enforced nation's laws and rescued people in trouble on waterways. Conducted search and rescue operations. Inspected ships of all sizes, from smallest watercraft to largest tankers to ensure seaworthiness and compliance with U.S. laws. Used advanced electronics, telecommunications, and computer systems.

DAMAGE CONTROL OFFICER / MAINTENANCE AND EMERGENCY REPAIR SPECIALIST. Maintained watertight integrity of Coast Guard vessels and emergency equipment used for firefighting and flooding. Performed plumbing repairs and welding fabrication and repairs. Inspected vessels for chemical, biological, and nuclear warfare. Trained in decontamination procedures.

EDUCATION

Albany Community College, Albany, NY; 23 quarter hours; 2004-2005

PROFESSIONAL TRAINING

Force Protection Fundamentals, Ship Board Security Engagement Weapons
Incident Response to Terrorist Bombings Awareness, Small Arms Instructor
Damage Control Personal Qualifications Standards
Intelligence Photography Course
Life Saving Equipment Manager
First Responder Awareness
Hazardous Materials
Gunner's Mate "A" School; Yorktown, Virginia: Trained in electronics and mechanical systems and with hydraulics; 10 weeks; 2005

PROFESSIONAL LICENSE: Captain's License – 50 ton

COMPUTER PROFICIENCIES: Microsoft Word, Excel, Access, PowerPoint

JASON JACKSON -- HIRED!
INTERNSHIP
Department of Navy
US Navy, E-5

BS Candidate, Security / Criminology

USAJOBS Upload Format

JASON JACKSON

5515 East-West Highway, #6 • Tallahassee, FL 32466
Cell: 850-777-8888 • Email: Jason.jackson@mac.com

OBJECTIVE: To obtain an entry-level position in the federal government in criminal justice, administration, or open-water investigative diving.

SUMMARY OF SKILLS

- Knowledgeable in criminology terminology and applications
- Certified International Association of Nitrox and Technical Divers (IANTD)
- Able to create legal documents including interrogatories, complaints, depositions, and contracts
- Skilled in maintaining and updating filing, inventory, and mailing, both manually and electronically
- Adept in operating photocopiers and scanners, facsimile machines, and personal computers
- Technology oriented; proficient in Microsoft Office programs
- Fluent in English and American Sign Language
- Resourceful, detail oriented, quick learner, flexible and self-disciplined
- Type 50+ words per minute

EDUCATION

Bachelor of Science (in progress), Public Safety and Security/Criminology, Minor: Underwater Crime Scene Investigation, Florida State University, Panama City Campus, Panama City, FL; Graduation anticipated: 05/2014

Relevant Criminology Courses:
Criminal Delinquent Behaviors; Criminalistics; Juvenile Justice; Religion and Crimes; Crime and Media; Crime Detectives and Investigation; Introduction to Underwater Investigation (and Lab); Drugs in the Justice System
- Expected to complete the Underwater Crime Scene Investigation Program 12/2013. Program focuses on underwater forensic investigations. Courses include application of theory and methodology relevant to many careers in law enforcement and public safety, as well as Underwater Crime Scene Methodology, Underwater Crime Scene Investigation, Forensic Science in Investigation, Science and Nitrox Dive Certification, and Technical Dive Certification.

Papers / Projects:
- Research: "Journal of Chrysalises in Criminalistics," a journal style report modeled after professional case reports and focused on lab examinations based on forensics and ballistics
- Research paper: "The Underwater Search and Evidence Response Team, Division of the FBI," an in-depth look at the careers of FBI dive team members and their job responsibilities

Activities:
Student Government Council, 01/2013-present
Lambda Alpha Epsilon (criminal justice fraternity), Sergeant at Arms, Board Member, 09/2010-present
Scuba, Hyperbaric, and Recreational Club (SHARC), 06/2011-present: club coordinates SCUBA training and organizes diving-related recreational activities for members with emphasis on safety

Scholarships:
- General Endowment Scholarship, 05/2011; selected to receive scholarship by committee in recognition for being a degree-seeking student who has maintained a 2.5 GPA or higher.
- Theodore R. and Vivian M. Johnson Scholarship, 08/2010; received this competitively awarded scholarship in recognition of my academic achievements as a disabled undergraduate student.

Associate of the Arts, General Liberal Arts, Gulf Coast State College, Panama City, FL, 05/2010

CERTIFICATIONS

International Association of Nitrox and Technical Divers (IANTD) Advanced Open Water Dive Certification, 06/2011
Sport Pilot License, 2011-present

WORK EXPERIENCE

Administrative Assistant, NG-303-1   07/2012 - 10/2012
Department of the Navy, Panama City, FL
40 hours/week; $10.27/hour
Supervisor: Shelly Smith, 850-444-5555. May be contacted.

PROCUREMENT SUPPORT: Entered purchase requests into automated Enterprise Resource Planning database for all Navy departments at NSWC Panama City, including small purchase card orders, government supply orders and contracts for labor and materials. Created routine purchase requisitions (PR) and tracked purchase orders to ensure materials and services were delivered as requested. Reviewed requests and input correct information; researched missing or incorrect information. Verified and ensured correct data entry, coding and forms. Provided end users with feedback to ensure on-time delivery of materials/services. Helped resolve error rate associated with inaccurate purchase requests.

ADMINISTRATIVE / OFFICE SUPPORT: Using judgment, chose the most appropriate reference material to relate to purchase; communicated with subject matter experts on issues not covered by reference materials. Used oral and written communication skills to resolve issues. Created and maintained file system to maintain PR documents generated.

KEY ACCOMPLISHMENT
Created 77 purchase orders for Milstrip and P-Cards in seven days with a 94 percent approval rate.

Flow Team Associate   08/2010 - Present
Target
2340 Highway 77, Panama City, FL 32405
30 hours/week, Salary: $8.75/hour
Supervisor: John Green, 850-777-8888. May be contacted.

UTILIZED ORGANIZATIONAL SKILLS in stocking and organizing merchandise throughout large retail store to maintain shelves' appearance and product availability. Took inventory; examined merchandise to identify and document items to be reordered or replenished. Assembled bicycles when requested.

DEMONSTRATED INTERPERSONAL SKILLS, politely and professionally worked with all levels of coworkers and management.

Laborer, WG-3502-05   05/2009 - 09/2009
Department of the Air Force, 325th Security Forces Unit Tyndall AFB, FL 32403
40 hours/week, Salary: $10.27/hour
Supervisor: Bonnie Austin, 850-222-3333. May be contacted.

PERFORMED critical functions such as inventory, packing, checkout, and loading/unloading of deployable personal equipment supporting Air Force units during deployments into high-risk locations. Provided administrative support supervisors; assisted with deployment processes and maintained reports.

Maintenance Repairman   08/2007 - 04/2008
Jacobson State Veterans Nursing Home, Port Charlotte, FL 33954
25 hours/week, Salary: $9.00/hour
Supervisor: Richard Olney, 850-777-8888. Please do not contact.

PERFORMED VARIOUS MAINTENANCE DUTIES; cleaned and maintained facility. Painted, pressure-washed, replaced A/C filters, and made general repairs. Made repairs to medical equipment such as wheelchairs and hospital beds for residents. Monitored and completed any repairs necessary to maintain proper safety and functioning of the facility.

Records Clerk   05/2005 - 05/2007
Federal Title Services, Panama City, FL 32405
40 hours/week, Salary: $13.55/hour
Supervisor: Carol Reilly, 850-555-6666. May be contacted.

ELECTRONICALLY ORGANIZED thousands of records by scanning paper documents to computer to update several years' documents. Filed and maintained records according to company policy.

DEMONSTRATED SUPERIOR TECHNICAL SKILLS using Microsoft Office applications and proprietary DocStar document management systems and LandAmerica database program software. Created a barcode and titling system for documents to be tracked electronically in a database system that assisted employees and the organization in expediting daily procedures and process of documents. Assisted coworkers with computer challenges.

EXCELLED IN WRITTEN COMMUNICATION; typed and issued homeowner, commercial, and lenders insurance policies. Reviewed and finalized correspondence and documents prepared by others demonstrating knowledge of correct grammar, spelling, capitalization, punctuation, and appropriate format.

Underwriter Clerk and Filing Clerk   08/1999 - 12/2001
Federal Title Insurance, Panama City, FL 32405
30 hours/week, Salary: $7.50/hour
Supervisor: Frank Shields, 850-888-9999. May be contacted.

COMPOSED CORRESPONDENCE, OFFICIAL DOCUMENTATION, checklists, reports, and other written materials. Typed and issued homeowner, commercial, and lenders policies through the use of a database computer program while gaining knowledge of title insurance.

PROVIDED ADMINISTRATIVE SUPPORT. Used organizational skills, filed and maintained records and documents while assisting staff with computer issues and needs.

EFFECTIVELY PLANNED AND ORGANIZED WORK. Analyzed problems to identify significant factors, gathered pertinent data, and provided solutions.

REFERENCES

Frank Shields, Owner and Manager
Federal Title Insurance
Panama City, FL
850-888-9999; email:

Romaine Thomas, Sign Language Interpreter
Florida State University Panama City
Panama City, FL
850-222-3333; email:

Timothy King, Ph.D., Criminology Advisor
Florida State University Panama City
Panama City, FL
850-777-0000; email: tking2@pc.fsu.edu

JASON JACKSON -- HIRED!
INTERNSHIP
Department of Navy
US Navy, E-5
> BS Candidate, Security / Criminology

Traditional Paper Format: 2-Page Private Industry Resume
Target: Criminal Justice / Open-Water Investigative Diving

JASON JACKSON
5515 East-West Highway, #6 • Tallahassee, FL 32466
Cell: 850-777-8888 • Email: Jason.jackson@mac.com

OBJECTIVE: To obtain an entry-level position in criminal justice or open-water investigative diving.

CERTIFICATIONS

International Association of Nitrox and Technical Divers (IANTD) Advanced Open Water Dive Certification, 06/2011
Sport Pilot License, 2011-present

EDUCATION

Bachelor of Science, expected May 2014
Major: Public Safety and Security/Criminology
Minor: Underwater Crime Scene Investigation
Florida State University, Panama City Campus, Panama City, FL

- **Expected to complete the Underwater Crime Scene Investigation Program 12/2013**. Program focuses on underwater forensic investigations. Courses include application of theory and methodology relevant to many careers in law enforcement and public safety.
- In addition to courses completed, the program offers more certifications through the completion of the program and the following courses:
  > Scientific Underwater Investigation; expect to receive Science and Nitrox dive certification
  > Forensic Science in Investigation; expect to receive Technical dive certification
  > Underwater Crime Scene Methodology
  > Underwater Crime Scene Investigation

Relevant Criminology Courses:
> Criminal Delinquent Behaviors; Criminalistics; Juvenile Justice; Religion and Crimes; Crime and Media; Crime Detectives and Investigation; Introduction to Underwater Investigation (and Lab); Drugs in the Justice System

Papers / Projects:
- Research: "Journal of Chrysalises in Criminalistics"
- Research paper: "The Underwater Search and Evidence Response Team, Division of the FBI."

WORK EXPERIENCE

Administrative Assistant, NG-303-1   07/2012 - 10/2012
Department of the Navy, Panama City, FL
40 hours/week; $10.27/hour

- PROCUREMENT SUPPORT: Entered purchase requests into automated Enterprise Resource Planning database for all Navy departments at NSWC Panama City, including small purchase card orders, government supply orders and contracts for labor and materials. Created routine purchase requisitions (PR) and tracked purchase orders to ensure materials and services were delivered as requested. Created 77 purchase orders for Milstrip and P-Cards in seven days with a 94 percent approval rate.

Flow Team Associate   08/2010 - Present
Target, Panama City, FL

- INVENTORY MAINTENANCE: stocked and organized inventory throughout large retail store to maintain shelves' appearance and product availability. Took inventory; examined merchandise to identify and document items to be reordered or replenished. Assembled bicycles when requested.

Laborer   05/2009 - 09/2009
Department of the Air Force, 325th Security Forces Unit Tyndall AFB, FL

- EQUIPMENT SUPPORT: maintained inventory, packing, checkout, and loading/unloading of deployable personal equipment supporting Air Force units during deployments into high-risk locations. Provided administrative support supervisors; assisted with deployment processes and maintained reports.

Maintenance Repairman   08/2007 - 04/2008
Jacobson State Veterans Nursing Home, Port Charlotte, FL

- MAINTENANCE DUTIES: cleaned and maintained facility. Painted, pressure-washed, replaced A/C filters, and made general repairs. Made repairs to medical equipment such as wheelchairs and hospital beds for residents. Monitored and completed any repairs necessary to maintain proper safety and functioning of the facility.

Records Clerk   05/2005 - 05/2007
Federal Title Services, Panama City, FL

- RECORDS MANAGEMENT: maintained thousands of records by scanning paper documents to computer to update several years' documents. Filed and maintained records according to company policy.

JASON JACKSON -- HIRED!
INTERNSHIP
Department of Navy
US Navy, E-5

BS Candidate, Security / Criminology

Traditional Paper Format: 2-Page Private Industry Resume
Target: Administrative / Records Management / Customer Services

JASON JACKSON

5515 East-West Highway, #6 • Tallahassee, FL 32466
Cell: 850-777-8888 • Email: Jason.jackson@mac.com

OBJECTIVE: To obtain an entry-level position in administration, records-management and customer services

SUMMARY OF SKILLS

- Able to create legal documents including interrogatories, complaints, depositions, and contracts.
- Technology Oriented
- Proficient in Microsoft Office Programs
- Type 50+ words per minute
- Skilled in maintaining and updating filing, inventory, and mailing, both manually and electronically.
- Adept in the operation of photocopiers and scanners, facsimile machines, and personal computers
- Resourceful, detail oriented, quick learner, flexible and self-disciplined

EDUCATION

Bachelor of Science, expected May 2014
Florida State University, Panama City Campus, Panama City, FL

ACTIVITIES:
Elected Student Council Representative, Fall 2013

SCHOLARSHIPS:
Theodore R. and Vivian M. Johnson Scholarship, August 18, 2010
General Endowment Scholarship, May 13, 2011.

WORK EXPERIENCE

Administrative Assistant   07/2012 - 10/2012
Department of the Navy, Panama City, FL
PROCUREMENT SUPPORT:
- Created 77 purchase orders in seven days with a 94 percent approval rate.
- Entered purchase requests into automated Enterprise Resource Planning database for all Navy departments at NSWC Panama City, including small purchase card orders, government supply orders and contracts for labor and materials.

- Created routine purchase requisitions (PR) and tracked purchase orders to ensure materials and services were delivered as requested. Reviewed requests and input correct information; researched missing or incorrect information.
- Verified and ensured correct data entry, coding and forms. Provided end users with feedback to ensure on-time delivery of materials/services. Helped resolve error rate associated with inaccurate purchase requests.

ADMINISTRATIVE / OFFICE SUPPORT:
- Utilized reference material to relate to purchase; communicated with customers concerning complex requests.
- Created and maintained file system to maintain documents generated.
- Proficient with database and product research, email communication and report generation.

Flow Team Associate   08/2010 - Present
Target, Panama City, FL
INVENTORY MAINTENANCE
- Stocked and organized inventory throughout large retail store to maintain shelves' appearance and product availability.
- Took inventory; examined merchandise to identify and document items to be reordered or replenished.

Records Clerk   05/2005 - 05/2007
Federal Title Services, Panama City, FL
RECORDS MANAGEMENT:
- Organized thousands of records by scanning paper documents to computer to update several years' documents.
- Filed and maintained records according to company policy.
- Utilized Microsoft Office applications and proprietary DocStar document management systems and LandAmerica database program software.
- Created a barcode and titling system for documents to be tracked electronically in a database system that assisted employees and the organization in expediting daily procedures and processing of documents. Assisted coworkers with computer challenges.

CORRRESPONDENCE:
- Typed and issued homeowner, commercial, and lenders insurance policies.
- Reviewed and finalized correspondence and documents prepared by others demonstrating knowledge of correct grammar, spelling, capitalization, punctuation, and appropriate format.

Underwriter Clerk and Filing Clerk   08/1999-12/2001
Lawyers Title Insurance, Panama City, FL
CORRESPONDENCE AND RECORDS MANAGEMENT:
- Produced checklists, reports, and other written materials.
- Typed and issued homeowner, commercial, and lenders policies through the use of a database computer program while gaining knowledge of title insurance.
- Used organizational skills, filed and maintained records and documents while assisting staff with computer issues and needs.

MARISOL MENDEZ -- HIRED!
PRESIDENTIAL MANAGEMENT FELLOWS
Army National Guard, E-5
  Master of Public Policy

USAJOBS Upload Format

MARISOL MENDEZ
1111 Mystery Lane
Baltimore, MD 21228
Phone: 333-333-3333
Email: Marisol.mendez111@gmail.com

OBJECTIVE: Presidential Management Fellow and/or National Security Policy Internship utilizing Master's in Public Policy and seven years in National Guard experience. Army National Guard, Honorably Discharged, E-5. Veteran's Preference: 10 points for 30 percent or more disability.

EDUCATION

Master's in Public Policy, expected Dec. 2012
Trachtenburg School, George Washington University, Washington, DC
GI Bill and Yellow Ribbon Scholarships

Concentration: National Security Policy. The national security policy field embraces processes of policy-making for national security, the analysis of defense programs, defense economics, the history of warfare and strategy, and the identification and understanding of the national and international security agenda in the 21st century.

Major courses:
ECON 6239: **Economics of National Defense**
HIST 6032: **Seminar on Strategy and Policy**
PSC 6348: **Politics of U.S. National Security Policy**
PSC 6349: **International Security Politics**

MAJOR PAPER: **Seminar on Strategy and Policy: 2002-2004 Analysis and Strategic Plans for the Transition of Guard Readiness and Return to Reserve Status.** Explored the OEF and OIF National Guard Readiness strategies from 2002-2004 to analyze trends and devise recommendations for return to Reserve Status. The thesis and recommendations provide National Guard Readiness policy-makers with a strategic plan for Reserve to Active to Reserve Duty with employment, career and educational planning tools.

2004, Bachelor's Degree, University of Ohio, Dayton, Ohio, Major: Business Administration (27 hours in business courses), GPA, 3.27 out of 4.0.

WORK HISTORY

09/2007 to 08/2010, READINESS NON-COMMISSIONED OFFICER, U.S. Army National Guard, Catonsville, MD; Honorably Discharged

- SENIOR ADVISOR AND ADMINISTERED mobilization readiness program to support unit personnel in preparation for changing deployment requirements.

- MANAGED ANALYTICAL AND EVALUATIVE STUDIES. Oversaw and monitored Military Occupational Specialty qualification program for unit personnel. Planned and coordinated Family Readiness Group activities.

- SUPERVISED AND LED activities of unit support staff and logistics personnel.

- ACCOMPLISHMENTS: Instrumental in preparing 60+ soldiers for deployment in support of Operation Iraqi Freedom. Initiated Family Readiness Group to support over 60 deployed personnel and their dependents; coordinated distribution of care packages to deployed soldiers. Assisted in coordination of deployment of 200 personnel and equipment in support of Operation Enduring Freedom; coordinated pre-deployment convoys to move unit's vehicles to deployment site. Planned and conducted training for 200 personnel.

05/2006 to 09/2007, PROPERTY BOOK NON-COMMISSIONED OFFICER, Maryland National Guard, Reisterstown, MD

- REVIEWED REQUESTS FOR, LOCATED, AND TRANSFERRED required equipment and gear for mobilizing units preparing for deployment, ensuring equipment readiness.

- USED AUTOMATED SYSTEMS, DATABASES AND COMPUTER APPLICATIONS. Prepared and generated unit reports for five battalions within Area Support Group. Verified unit equipment on hand in database, and match to monthly Unit Readiness List.

- ACCOMPLISHMENTS: Located available equipment and prepared documentation for equipment transfers for mobilizing units.

11/2005 to 05/2006, TRAINING NCO/ADMINISTRATOR, Maryland National Guard, 1008 Transportation Company, Reisterstown, MD.

Prepared 40+ unit personnel for deployment in support of Operation Iraqi Freedom. While working at Soldier Readiness Processing site, led team to process hundreds of personnel actions and meet deadlines for required daily processing.

AWARDS, HONORS, RECOGNITION

Global War on Terrorism Service Medal, 2006; Army Reserve Component Achievement Medal; National Defense Service Medal; Armed Forces Reserve Medal; Non-Commissioned Officer Professional Development Ribbon 3rd Award; Army Service Ribbon; Armed Forces Reserve Medal with M Device.

MARISOL MENDEZ -- HIRED!
PRESIDENTIAL MANAGEMENT FELLOWS
Army National Guard, E-5
Master of Public Policy

Harvard Format

MARISOL MENDEZ

1111 Mystery Lane
Baltimore, MD 21228
Phone: 333-333-3333
Email: Marisol.mendez111@gmail.com

OBJECTIVE: **Management Training Program** – Logistics, Transportation, Policy

EDUCATION   GEORGE WASHINGTON UNIVERSITY, Washington, DC
Trachtenberg School
Master's in Public Policy, expected Dec. 2013
GI Bill and Yellow Ribbon Scholarships

Concentration: **National Security Policy.** The national security policy field embraces processes of policy-making for national security, the analysis of defense programs, defense economics, the history of warfare and strategy, and the identification and understanding of the national and international security agenda in the 21st century.

Major courses: ECON 6239: **Economics of National Defense**
HIST 6032: **Seminar on Strategy and Policy**
PSC 6348: **Politics of U.S. National Security Policy**
PSC 6349: **International Security Politics**

Major Paper   **Seminar on Strategy and Policy: 2002-2004 Analysis and Strategic Plans for the Transition of Guard Readiness and Return to Reserve Status.** Explored the OEF and OIF National Guard Readiness strategies from 2002-2004 to analyze trends and devise recommendations for return to Reserve Status. The thesis and recommendations provide National Guard Readiness policy-makers with a strategic plan for Reserve to Active to Reserve Duty with employment, career and educational planning tools.

UNIVERSITY OF DAYTON, Dayton, Ohio
Bachelor's Degree, 2005
Major: Business Administration (27 hours in business courses)
GPA, 3.27 out of 4.0.

WORK HISTORY   **US ARMY NATIONAL GUARD, Catonsville, MD, 9/2008 to 8/2011**

READINESS NON-COMMISSIONED OFFICER
Honorably Discharged

SENIOR ADVISOR AND ADMINISTERED mobilization readiness program to support unit personnel in preparation for changing deployment requirements.

- MANAGED ANALYTICAL AND EVALUATIVE STUDIES. Oversaw and monitored Military Occupational Specialty qualification program for unit personnel. Planned and coordinated Family Readiness Group activities.

- SUPERVISED AND LED activities of unit support staff and logistics personnel.

ACCOMPLISHMENTS:
- Instrumental in preparing 60+ soldiers for deployment in support of Operation Iraqi Freedom. Initiated Family Readiness Group to support over 60 deployed personnel and their dependents; coordinated distribution of care packages to deployed soldiers.
- Assisted in coordination of deployment of 200 personnel and equipment in support of Operation Enduring Freedom; coordinated pre-deployment convoys to move unit's vehicles to deployment site. Planned and conducted training for 200 personnel.

MARYLAND NATIONAL GUARD, Reisterstown, MD
Property Book Non-Commissioned Officer, 05/2006 to 09/2007

- REVIEWED REQUESTS FOR, LOCATED, AND TRANSFERRED required equipment and gear for mobilizing units preparing for deployment, ensuring equipment readiness.

- USED AUTOMATED SYSTEMS, DATABASES AND COMPUTER APPLICATIONS. Prepared and generated unit reports for five battalions within Area Support Group. Verified unit equipment on hand in database, and match to monthly Unit Readiness List.

- ACCOMPLISHMENTS: Located available equipment and prepared documentation for equipment transfers for mobilizing units.

MARYLAND NATIONAL GUARD, Reisterstown, MD
Training NCO / Administrator, 11/2005 to 05/2006
1008 Transportation Company

Prepared 40+ unit personnel for deployment in support of Operation Iraqi Freedom. While working at Soldier Readiness Processing site, led team to process hundreds of personnel actions and meet deadlines for required daily processing.

AWARDS: Global War on Terrorism Service Medal, 2006; Army Reserve Component Achievement Medal; National Defense Service Medal; Armed Forces Reserve Medal; Non-Commissioned Officer Professional Development Ribbon 3rd Award; Army Service Ribbon; Armed Forces Reserve Medal with M Device.

COVER LETTER FOR A PERMANENT POSITION

RACHEL BELL
1234 Doorpost Rd
College Park, MD 20741
Cell: 443-333-3333 | rachelbell@email.com

April 2011
Ms. Almaz Beyene
Headquarters
HC-32, Headquarters Special Programs
Washington, DC 20585

Dear Ms. Beyene:

I am writing to apply for the New Media Specialist position (job announcement #: DOE-HQ-11-SCEP-HC-00154) posted on USA Jobs. In our current global position, the Department of Energy is an agency that plays a key role in influencing energy use and technologies on both a national and global level. By working in the Office of the Chief Human Capital Officer, one would have opportunities to recruit and maintain the best talent for the Department of Energy who will be the innovators of energy technology.

As a recent graduate from the University of Maryland with significant experience in social media, web 2.0 applications, and publishing information for the general public, I would be a great fit in the position of New Media Specialist. Due to my background as an English major, I bring the written and oral communication skills necessary to draft, publish and manage content on social media services such as Twitter, Facebook, and LinkedIn.

As a current intern at the Department of Energy, I have had many experiences with using social media and virtual worlds for recruitment purposes. These skills and experiences prepare me to be a great asset to the Department of Energy Office of the Chief Human Capital Officer.

I am excited to continue my efforts with the DOE team as the Department expands to new and innovative uses of social media. Thank you for your time and consideration.

Sincerely,

Rachel Bell

Enclosure: Résumé

PRESIDENTIAL MANAGEMENT FELLOWS COVER LETTER

MARISOL MENDEZ
1111 Mystery Lane
Baltimore, MD 21228
Email: Marisol.mendez111@gmail.com
May 20, 2010

Presidential Management Fellows Program
Address
City, State, Zipcode

Re: PRESIDENTIAL MANAGEMENT FELLOWSHIP

Dear Presidential Management Fellows Program Recruiter:

I would like to begin my federal civilian career as a Presidential Management Fellow and pursue a rotation and eventual career with the Office of the Secretary of Defense and the National Guard Bureau at the Pentagon. My career mission is to contribute to the development of efficient and effective policies, programs and workforce planning for National Guard programs.

I am currently completing my MPP in Dec. 2012 and am concentrating in National Security Policy. My Senior paper emphasizes the Analysis and Strategic Plans for the Transition of Guard Readiness and Return to Reserve Status.

I have served in the National Guard as an Operations Manager with specialization in administration, property, training, and readiness for the past five years.

My military specialized expertise includes:
• Leading evaluative studies to support changing Guard requirements for readiness, materials, and administration.
• Knowledge of and skill in analytical and evaluative methods to improve efficiency and effectiveness of the Guard program operations.

I would like the opportunity to provide my administrative, analytical, and communications skills to the Office of Secretary of Defense PMF Rotation.

Sincerely,
Marisol Mendez

Attachments: Federal Resume, DD214, other PMF attachments

INTERNSHIP COVER LETTER

SCOTT HAMPSTEAD
5555 University Boulevard | Hyattsville, MD 20783
Phone: 410-333-3333
Email: scottmhampstead@hotmail.com

Date
Name of Agency
Department
Street Address
City, State, Zip
Re: Job Title, Announcement

Dear Mr./Ms. _____:

I am writing to express my interest in the intern position with the Army Corps of Engineers. I learned of this opportunity through the Civilian Personnel Advisory Center in Washington, DC., where I was told that you would be the person to contact for more information on internship opportunities.

I recently graduated from the University of Maryland at College Park with a B.S. in Mechanical Engineering. My GPA is 3.65/4.0 overall and 3.75/4.0 in engineering classes. I am particularly interested in the Outstanding Scholars and Internship Programs through USACE.

I would like to utilize some of the following skills with the Army Corps of Engineers:
1. Knowledge of part/assembly creation, modeling and manufacturing in Pro-Engineer CAD software.
2. Product design skills including test design, research and analysis, and prototype construction.
3. General understanding of engineering principles from my University of Maryland education.
4. Writing, research and analysis for projects.
5. Experience as a team leader and team member for many design and engineering projects.

I have attached my Federal resume for your review. If you need any other information, or could steer me to any specific vacancy announcements, please contact me.

I appreciate your time and consideration with my application.

Thank you very much.

INTERNSHIP COVER LETTER

JEREMY D. DENTON
1234 Anywhere Street
City, State, Zipcode
Phone: 555.555.5555
Email: jeremy.d.denton@gmail.com

May 14, 2011

Government Printing Office
Human Capital Operations
732 North Capitol Street NW, Room A-638
Washington, DC 20401

Dear Ms. Howard:

Enclosed is my application responding to Vacancy Announcement # 10-346057-rm, Recent Graduate (Pathways), Management and Program Analyst position.

I can offer the Office of Human Capital of the GPO proven Management and Program Analysis expertise, together with a **Bachelor of Arts degree in Government and Public Policy**, plus strong executive leadership experience in the following areas:

Critical Thinking, Analysis, and Problem-Solving – Experienced short- and long-term project analyst, with field experience in using evaluative and technical skills to analyze and optimize operations quickly and decisively.

Work Planning, Organization, and Management – Assisted in the supervision and administration of essential aircraft maintenance operations, including at remote, challenging locations. Developed methods and procedures to improve efficiency of the Flight Crew, especially in flight operations or emergency maintenance procedures.

Leadership – 5 years with the US Marine Corps as a highly effective, successful, decorated sergeant and project leader able to direct multiple events under extreme pressure, including in combat situations.

I would like to have the opportunity to offer my extensive experience to the GPO Human Capital Office. I look forward to the opportunity to meet in person for an interview.

Thank you for your consideration of my application materials

Sincerely,
Jeremy D. Denton

Enclosures: Federal Resume

INTERNSHIP COVER LETTER

Brandon Billings
304 Aalapapa Drive
Kailua, HI 96734
(808) 222-2222
Brandon.billings@gmail.com
May 10, 2010

Human Capital Operations Division,
Attn: FLETC Intern Program Coordinator
1131 Chapel Crossing Road, Townhouse 393
Glynco, GA 31524

To whom it may concern:

Please find enclosed my Internship Resume for consideration of the College Intern Program at the Federal Law Enforcement Center at Glynco, GA.

My relevant qualifications include:
- Current full-time position pursuing BS in Homeland Security with emphasis in Law Enforcement at Embry-, Riddle Aeronautical University, Schofield Barracks, HI. I am completing 12 credit hours and will complete my degree in May 2014.
- Three years specialized experience in security officer and harbor patrol with the U.S. Coast Guard as a Boarding Team Member.
- My experience includes law enforcement and investigation of cases, such as smugglers and illegal entrants.
- I would be an asset to the internship program because:
- I have one year specialized experience in law enforcement operation practices and techniques.
- I have experience in criminal investigative case development.
- My training in Microsoft and skill in writing reports will be an asset as a Police Officer and investigative agent.

Thank you for your time and consideration. I look forward to your response.

Sincerely,
Brandon Billings

Enclosures
Internship resume, FETC Intern Nomination Form, FLETC College Intern Program
Application and Narrative Essay, Proof of requirement for credit; Official college transcripts, OF-306; DD-214

Addendum

⇢ Federal Student Loan Repayment Program
⇢ Federal Job Benefits and Internship Perks
⇢ Using the Schedule A Authority

SAMPLE PATHWAYS ANNOUNCEMENT

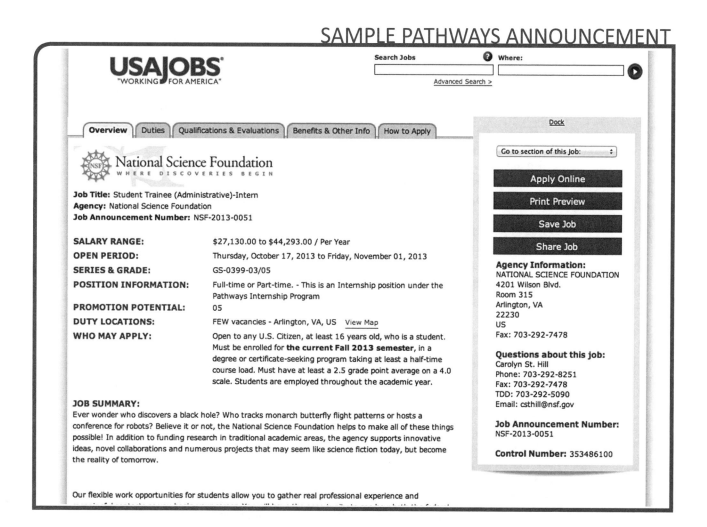

USAJOBS®
"WORKING FOR AMERICA"

Search Jobs   Where:
Advanced Search >

| Overview | Duties | Qualifications & Evaluations | Benefits & Other Info | How to Apply |

National Science Foundation
WHERE DISCOVERIES BEGIN

Job Title: Student Trainee (Administrative)-Intern
Agency: National Science Foundation
Job Announcement Number: NSF-2013-0051

SALARY RANGE:	$27,130.00 to $44,293.00 / Per Year
OPEN PERIOD:	Thursday, October 17, 2013 to Friday, November 01, 2013
SERIES & GRADE:	GS-0399-03/05
POSITION INFORMATION:	Full-time or Part-time. - This is an Internship position under the Pathways Internship Program
PROMOTION POTENTIAL:	05
DUTY LOCATIONS:	FEW vacancies - Arlington, VA, US View Map
WHO MAY APPLY:	Open to any U.S. Citizen, at least 16 years old, who is a student. Must be enrolled for **the current Fall 2013 semester**, in a degree or certificate-seeking program taking at least a half-time course load. Must have at least a 2.5 grade point average on a 4.0 scale. Students are employed throughout the academic year.

JOB SUMMARY:
Ever wonder who discovers a black hole? Who tracks monarch butterfly flight patterns or hosts a conference for robots? Believe it or not, the National Science Foundation helps to make all of these things possible! In addition to funding research in traditional academic areas, the agency supports innovative ideas, novel collaborations and numerous projects that may seem like science fiction today, but become the reality of tomorrow.

Our flexible work opportunities for students allow you to gather real professional experience and

Dock

Go to section of this Job:

Apply Online

Print Preview

Save Job

Share Job

Agency Information:
NATIONAL SCIENCE FOUNDATION
4201 Wilson Blvd.
Room 315
Arlington, VA
22230
US
Fax: 703-292-7478

Questions about this job:
Carolyn St. Hill
Phone: 703-292-8251
Fax: 703-292-7478
TDD: 703-292-5090
Email: csthill@nsf.gov

Job Announcement Number:
NSF-2013-0051

Control Number: 353486100

Federal Student Loan Repayment Program

If you get a federal job offer, negotiate for student loan repayment.

The Federal student loan repayment program permits agencies to repay federally insured student loans as a recruitment or retention incentive for candidates or current employees of the agency.

Employee Coverage
Any employee (as defined in 5 U.S.C. 2105) is eligible, except those occupying a position excepted from the competitive civil service because of their confidential, policy-determining, policy-making, or policy-advocating nature (e.g., Schedule C appointees).

Loans Eligible for Payment
Loans eligible for payment are those made, insured, or guaranteed under parts B, D, or E of title IV of the Higher Education Act of 1965 or a health education assistance loan made or insured under part A of title VII or part E of title VIII of the Public Health Service Act. (See Q&A 17 See the OPM website, *www.opm.gov/policy-data-oversight/pay-leave/student-loan-repayment/*, for examples of the types of student loans that are eligible for repayment.)

Limitations
Although the student loan is not forgiven, agencies may make payments to the loan holder of up to a maximum of $10,000 for an employee in a calendar year and a total of not more than $60,000 for any one employee.

Discretionary Authority
As with any incentive, this authority is used at the discretion of the agency. Because the authority is discretionary, agencies may have different approaches or policies relating to student loan repayment. Make sure you research individual agency policies.

Service Agreement
An employee receiving this benefit must sign a service agreement to remain in the service of the paying agency for a period of at least 3 years. An employee must reimburse the paying agency for all benefits received if he or she is separated voluntarily or separated involuntarily for misconduct, unacceptable performance, or a negative suitability determination under 5 CFR part 731. In addition, an employee must maintain an acceptable level of performance in order to continue to receive repayment benefits.

Forgive any Remaining Debt after 10 Years of Public Service
Public service workers – such as teachers, nurses, and those in military service – will see any remaining debt forgiven after 10 years. More information can be found at: *www.whitehouse.gov/issues/education/higher-education/ensuring-that-student-loans-are-affordable*

Periods in a Non-Pay Status
Periods of leave without pay, or other periods during which the employee is not in a pay status, do not count toward completion of the required service period. The service completion date must be extended by the total amount of time spent in non-pay status. However, absence because of uniformed service or compensable injury is considered creditable toward the required service period upon reemployment.

Federal Job Benefits and Internship Perks

Federal workers enjoy top-flight benefits.

Federal government employees enjoy a wide range of "family-friendly" benefits that go far beyond insurance and retirement. Each agency is free to offer its own benefits package. The following is a sample of the benefits available to permanent Federal employees.

- *Leave and Holidays:*
  13 days sick leave each year; 13, 20, or 26 days of vacation leave each year, depending on years of service; 10 days paid holiday each year.

- *Federal Employees Retirement System (FERS):*
  Benefits based on amount of service and salary history.

- *Student Loan Repayment:*
  Permits agencies to repay the student loans of federal employees; used at the discretion of the agency.

- *Thrift Savings Plan (TSP):*
  Multiple investment options similar to a 401(k) plan.

- *Federal Employees Health Benefits Program (FEHB):*
  No waiting periods, required medical exam, or age/physical condition restrictions.

- *Federal Employees Group Life Insurance (FEGLI):*
  Group term life insurance: basic life insurance and three options (Standard, Additional, and Family).

- *Family Friendly Leave Flexibility:*
  Flexible work schedules, telecommuting, family friendly leave policies, Employee Assistance Program (EAP), part-time and job sharing positions, child and elder care resources, adoption information/incentives, and child support services.

- *Work/Life Programs:*
  Every federal agency has an Employee Assistance Program (EAP), which has a goal to restore employees to full productivity. More specifically, the EAP provides free, confidential short-term counseling to identify the employee's problem and, when appropriate, make a referral to an outside organization, facility, or program that can assist the employee in resolving his or her problem.

- *Recruitment Bonus:*
  Lump-sum bonus to newly appointed employees for difficult-to-fill positions. Up to 25% of basic pay may be paid prior to employee starting position. Service agreement with repayment plan if service time not fulfilled.

- *Employee Development:*
  Career Resource Centers; Training Opportunities.

- *Child Care Subsidy Program:*
  Federal agencies, at their own discretion, can use appropriated funds, including revolving funds otherwise available for salaries, to assist lower income federal employees with the costs of child care.

Schedule A Federal Hiring Authority

In Executive Order 12548 of July 26, 2010, President Obama established a hiring increase goal of 100,000 people with disabilities into the federal government over five years, including individuals with targeted disabilities.

> *My administration is committed to ensuring people living with disabilities have*
> *fair access to jobs so they can contribute to our economy and realize their dreams.*
> *Individuals with disabilities are a vital and dynamic part of our Nation.*
> *--President Barack Obama, July, 2010*

Schedule A is an excepted service hiring authority available to federal agencies to hire and/or promote individuals with disabilities without competing for the job. Schedule A hiring authority allows federal agencies to avoid using the traditional, and sometimes lengthy, competitive hiring process.

Have positions been filled under Schedule A? Yes. Data available from the Office of Personnel Management reveals that the federal government employs more than 200,000 individuals with disabilities, more than 17,000 of whom are individuals with targeted disabilities. In FY 2011, the federal government hired more than 18,000 individuals with disabilities, comprising 14.7% of all new hires. (Source: Report on the Employment of Individuals with Disabilities in the Executive Branch – July 25, 2012)

Application Options for Those with Disabilities

Beyond simply applying without identifying yourself as disabled, you have 3 ways to disclose that you are a person with a disability:

1. Submit your application competitively for a position through USAJOBS (*www.usajobs. gov*), where approximately 20,000 federal jobs are posted daily. Identify yourself as disabled by checking off that you are authorized to be hired as person with a disability. Be prepared to build your resume if you have not already done so.

2. Directly contact the hiring manager for a position you have identified and send them a copy of your Schedule A Application.

3. Contact the Selective Placement Program Coordinator (SPPC) about particular openings. These hiring officials are on the lookout for talented employees who have disabilities. For a list of the coordinators, go to *www.opm.gov/disability/SSPCoord.asp*. For more on hiring through USAJOBS, go to *www.opm.gov/faq/USAJOBS/dfdfdfd.ashx*

4. NEW! Submit your resume to the WRP.gov database for students with disabilities. More than 20 federal government agencies regularly utilize the WRP as a recruiting source, with more than 6,500 students obtaining federal employment since 1995.

Why Do I Need a Schedule A Letter?

In order to apply with the disabled status under the special hiring authority, jobseekers must provide proof of a disability, and the Schedule A Letter satisfies that requirement. The Schedule A Letter confirming the disability should be signed by a licensed medical professional, state or private vocational rehabilitation specialist, or any government agency that issues or provides disability benefits. The letter often also notes your job readiness for the work you're seeking. Schedule A Letters are submitted through USAJOBS and are given to other federal hiring authorities. The letter should be brief and to the point, and should not go into details about the nature of your disability. Focus on your skills and experience that will be relevant for that agency's mission and services.

What Does a Schedule A Application Include?

Whether you are applying through USAJOBS or you are sending your application through e-mail to a Selective Placement Officer or hiring manager, the application will be made up of these documents:

⇢ Your own cover letter
⇢ Schedule A Letter
⇢ Federal resume
⇢ Transcript (if you are applying for positions with your education as a qualification)

You can upload the Schedule A Letter, cover letter, and transcripts into USAJOBS along with your resume. Alternatively, you can e-mail these documents separately as attached files to the Selective Placement Program Coordinator (SPPC).

About the Authors

Kathryn Troutman is a leading expert in federal jobs, a hot topic with the change of administration and the current downturn in the economy. She brings over 30 years of experience in this unique marketplace and has the ability to take the complex subject of federal job searching and break it down into understandable steps.

She is the author of *Ten Steps to a Federal Job,* now in its third edition. The first *Ten Steps* book was honored as the Best Career Guide of 2002 by the Publishers Marketing Association.

Troutman wrote the first book on the federal resume format in 1995 in response to the government's move to replace the cumbersome SF-171 form with the resume. These days, she is known as the "Federal Resume Guru," and her book, The *Federal Resume Guidebook*, is a best-seller and in its 4th printing. Over 100 US government agencies hire Troutman to speak as a master trainer each year, and her presentations on writing federal resumes are popular.

Troutman has been interviewed by both national print and electronic media outlets on how to get a job in the Federal (and Obama) administration. Troutman is also a columnist for eight online federal and military employment websites.

In addition, Troutman is a trainer's trainer. She has established two certification programs for career counselors on federal job searching. A licensed curriculum, based on her *Ten Steps*, is taught around the world. Troutman's message is that there are many desirable federal jobs, but you must know the right way to apply. Featured in the 2nd edition of *Ten Steps to a Federal Job* are 24 jobseekers who took her recommended steps and landed their dream jobs with Uncle Sam.

Besides federal employment, Troutman also with speaks passionately on "Staying Successful with a Small Business and Women Entrepreneurs." Troutman's firm, The Resume Place, has been in business for over 25 years, and she and the company continue to grow and evolve.

Paul Binkley has worked closely with students and professionals on federal careers, served on many panels on federal hiring, and developed workshops over the last ten years. Currently, he is the Education Human and Institutional Capacity Development Advisor with the U.S. Agency for International Development in Monrovia, Liberia. Prior to that, he was Director of Career Services at The George Washington University's (GWU) Trachtenberg School of Public Policy and Public Administration. As director, he provided services to over 450 Master of Public Administration, Master of Public Policy, Certificate of Nonprofit Management, and Doctor of Public Policy and Administration students. Binkley also worked with the over 3200 Trachtenberg School alumni to cultivate professional opportunities around the world and for their own professional development.

During his time at GWU, Binkley was involved with university-wide efforts to coordinate career services for all students and alumni. He helped establish the GW Career Centers Network and also served on the Presidential Career Services Task Force, which submitted its recommendations to GWU's President in April 2011.

Binkley's education and professional experiences have focused on higher education and international human capacity development. He completed a doctorate in higher education administration at GWU in 2012 and focused his research on how student involvement impacts graduate level alumni giving. He completed a Master's degree in Foreign Affairs and Diplomacy at the University of Kentucky's Patterson School of Diplomacy and International Commerce. His Bachelor's degree is from St. John's University of Minnesota.

Over the last few years, Binkley has also served as an elections monitor in such places as Azerbaijan, Tajikistan, and Macedonia. He spent several weeks in Kosovo and Iraq working with faculty, students, and government officials on higher education programs. He has also completed a certificate in Human Performance Improvement (HPI); is a Myers Briggs Type Indicator (MBTI) facilitator, certified Global Career Development Facilitator, and Certified Federal Job Search Trainer (CFJST); and hopes to become a Certified Performance Technologist in the near future.

Binkley is originally from central Minnesota and currently lives in Monrovia, Liberia.

Foreword by Paul Binkley

The more things change, the more they stay the same.

When we wrote the second edition of this book, the Pathways Programs were just beginning to come into focus. We knew that Pathways would be implemented, but didn't know exactly what the landscape would look like once that happened. Before Pathways, students had a pretty good shot at landing a federal position or internship, but achieving success required navigating a sometimes overwhelming number of hiring programs.

Today, Pathways is the law of the land – implemented via final rule on July 10, 2012 – and, with more than a year of observation, we now know the ins and outs of the new paradigm for student hiring within the federal government.

We fully acknowledge that with budget cuts, pay freezes, and scary sounding things like "furlough" and "sequestration," starting a career in the federal government has become more difficult over the last few years. And, in a struggling economy, many students and veterans who would otherwise be looking for private sector jobs have turned their eyes toward employment with the federal government, making the competition stiffer. This increased level of competition makes it even more important for students to take time and effort to understand how federal hiring works – and what will help get their applications to the top.

The suggestions, activities, tips and tricks found in this edition of the *Student's Federal Career Guide* remain effective and successful. The third edition of the *Student's Federal Career Guide* builds on the tried and true methods from earlier editions and gives you new ideas for how to identify and successfully apply to federal government jobs that truly interest you. Additionally, we lay out the details of the Pathways Programs, making it easy for you to understand the programs and how to create the strongest application possible.

The federal resume template in this edition provides you with the structure and content that work for any opportunities within the federal government, whether direct hire positions or components of the Pathways Programs. No longer will you need one resume for internships and another for full-time positions. Known as the Outline Format, this resume style gives you the flexibility to present prior work, internships, volunteer activities, class projects, or research papers as the experiences hiring managers are looking for.

It is critical that your applications are laser-focused on what each federal position demands. Federal human resource professionals and hiring managers must now review more applications than ever before, and it is in your best interest to make it easy for them to find the RIGHT information immediately. This book gives you the tools to do just that: to clearly show decision-makers that you have what they need.

Of course, the resume is only part of the process. Finding positions that match your interests and meet your personal and professional criteria is not an easy task, especially when much of the terminology used by the federal government remains vague.

Don't worry. We can help you with this process and much more.

Despite the recent changes in the student hiring landscape—particularly the implementation of Pathways—one could argue that not much has really changed over the last couple years. The federal government is still looking for talented, dedicated people like you. The competition to "get in" is still fierce. And we're still here to help. What you hold in your hands now remains one of the best resources for those serious about obtaining and building a satisfying public service career.

Paul Binkley, EdD
Monrovia, Liberia, September 2013

"*In today's world of danger and opportunity, there is no higher calling than public service. No other job affords you the chance to impact people's lives for the better, promote their safety and health, and open access to public services. From my own experience, I can attest to the satisfaction that Federal Service can bring to employees who know they are making a difference for the good in the lives of others. I hope [this book] helps open the door to this world and sheds light on the paths to the kind of satisfaction I took from my own career in Federal Service.*"

The Honorable Alvin P. Adams
Former Ambassador to Peru and Haiti

Acknowledgements

First, I would like to thank Paul Binkley for the insightful contributions and patient, continuous updating with the latest programs for students and recent graduates based on his experience as Director of Career Development Services at the Trachtenberg School of Public Policy and Public Administration, George Washington University. Paul has also created and has instructed excellent presentations for the CFJST / CFCC program for career counselors and military education counselors on federal internship programs for the past six years. I'm thankful to Emily Troutman, my daughter, for her writing and ideas for the first edition which is the basis of this third edition. Emmanuel Waters, former Intern and now Federal Civil Servant, contributed insight for intern applicants who are seeking positions in government. I appreciate his content and resume for this book. Thank you to Tamara Golden, Career Consultant, School of International Relations and Pacific Studies, University of California who hosted our Certified Federal Job Search Trainer program at the La Jolla Campus.

—*Kathryn Troutman, Co-Author, Publisher*

I would like to first thank Kathryn Troutman for inviting me to co-author the book and for being a tireless advocate for all those who want to serve in the federal government. I am thankful for the support I have received from the faculty, staff, students, and alumni of the Trachtenberg School, and the career services professionals around the world. I truly appreciate my colleagues in the National Association of Schools of Public Affairs and Administration (NASPAA) who have been an invaluable source of honest input, ideas, and insight. I am always amazed at how much they do with so few resources. Finally, I want to thank my close friends and my wife for their patience and understanding, even though it feels like they haven't seen me in a long, long time.

—*Paul Binkley, Co-Author*

Preface to the 3rd Edition by Kathryn Troutman

The 3rd edition of the *Student's Federal Career Guide* updates key information and adds new student-oriented advice not included in the previous two editions. The third edition is written for the same audience: all students who are part-time or full-time in college or graduate school; recent graduates (within the last two years); veterans who are using the GI Bill to return to college to begin a new career; and career changers who are going back to school to change career direction.

The purpose of the third edition is to update students and recent graduates on the federal government's Pathways Programs. Pursuant to a Final Rule published on July 10, 2012, the Pathways Programs— which include an internship program, a recent graduates program, and the Presidential Management Fellows Program—provide a roadmap for students seeking exposure to federal service and the possibility of a federal career.

Introducing all-new, up-to-date information on Federal Internships, Fellowships, and Student/Recent Graduate Hiring Programs. The third edition hones in on recent changes made to federal programs designed to recruit students and recent graduates. In this edition, these programs are demystified, with specific emphasis on clarifying eligibility requirements and enhancing your understanding of the application process.

Introducing updated resume formats and samples for internship applications and USAJOBS federal job applications. The second edition introduced two student-focused resume formats—one for internships and another for federal job applications. The third edition offers updated formats and samples to help guide you as you target competitive federal student programs.

This book is dedicated to helping students understand and follow the programs sponsored with the Pathways Program, which was created by President Obama's EXECUTIVE ORDER for RECRUITING AND HIRING STUDENTS AND RECENT GRADUATES, December 2010 , and implemented via the Final Rule on July 10, 2012.

> *"Section 1. Policy. The Federal Government benefits from a diverse workforce that includes students and recent graduates, who infuse the workplace with their enthusiasm, talents, and unique perspectives. The existing competitive hiring process for the*

Federal civil service, however, is structured in a manner that, even at the entry level, favors job applicants who have significant previous work experience. This structure, along with the complexity of the rules governing admission to the career civil service, creates a barrier to recruiting and hiring students and recent graduates. It places the Federal Government at a competitive disadvantage compared to private-sector employers when it comes to hiring qualified applicants for entry-level positions."
www.whitehouse.gov/the-press-office/2010/12/27/executive-order-recruiting-and-hiring-students-and-recent-graduates

Three things are mandatory to land one of the best internships and jobs in the country: perseverance, networking, and following the samples in this book.

Kathryn Troutman, Co-Author and Publisher,
Student's Federal Career Guide, 3rd Edition

Other Books by The Resume Place, Inc.

⇢ Ten Steps to a Federal Job & CD-ROM, 3rd Ed.
⇢ Military to Federal Career Guide, 2nd Ed.
⇢ Jobseeker's Guide, 5th Ed.
⇢ Federal Resume Guidebook & CD-ROM, 5th Ed.
  (Published by Jist, Inc., Indianapolis, IN)
⇢ The Student's Federal Career Guide, 2nd Ed. & CD-ROM
⇢ Creating Your High School Resume, 3rd Ed.
  (Published by Jist, Inc., Indianapolis, IN)

INDEX

Resume Place Federal Resume Sample Database™

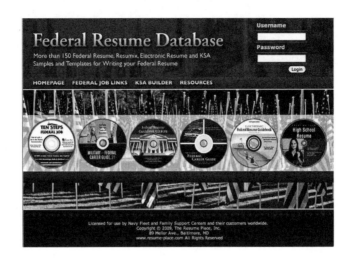

From ten of Kathryn Troutman's federal resume writing books and CD-ROMs, review samples of the best federal resumes to develop your own first draft and federal resume. Includes samples for over 50 occupational series and grades.

Over 400 outstanding, successful samples of federal resumes and KSAs from the following publications:

• Federal Resume Guidebook, 4th & 5th Editions
• Ten Steps to a Federal Job, 2nd & 3rd Editions
• Student's Federal Career Guide
• Jobseeker Guide, 3rd & 4th Editions
• Electronic Federal Resume Guidebook, 1st Edition
• Military to Federal Career Guide, 1st & 2nd Editions

License fee: $45.00 for a one year individual license.
Multi-user licenses are also available for military bases, federal agencies, universities, and career centers.
www.resume-place.com/certification-programs/online-federal-resume-database/

Get More Expert Help With Your Federal Application!

Federal Resume Writing Services by Certified Federal Resume Writers

Your federal resume is your most important federal career document. After you read this book and look at the samples, consider the professional services of expert federal career consultants and federal resume writers.

The Best Resume Format

Our signature Outline Format designed by Kathryn Troutman is preferred by federal human resources specialists, because they can easily find the information they are seeking.

Federal Career Consulting

Advice and recommendations on federal positions and occupational standards to match your experience, education, and specialized knowledge. Get the latest up-to-date strategies on how to market your past experience into new careers in government.

More Information:
www.resume-place.com
(888) 480-8265